Praise for *Cure for the Common Life*

"In these pages you will leave the common life in the dust. You will learn that each person was designed as a one-of-a-kind to achieve one certain purpose. You begin to experience the fact that God has embedded in your soul the power and passion to fulfill your purpose. It is a profound message for those who long for a unity of their belief and their life in this world."

> — Art Miller,
> founder of People Management
> International, Inc., and author of
> *The Power of Uniqueness*

"Max Lucado has done it again! This book is a jewel. I say that because he hits the nail on the head when he reveals in chapter after chapter that people cannot be anything they want to be but they can be everything God wants them to be. Read, discover, and rejoice in your sweet spot, out of which you are intended to live."

> — Millard Fuller,
> founder of Habitat for Humanity
> and The Fuller Center for Housing

"I recommend this book if you fall into any of these categories: you're working, parenting, calling the shots, serving, wondering, graduating, longing, breathing. Your focus will be refined. Your battery will be recharged."

> — Ernie Johnson Jr.,
> sportscaster for TNT

"Max Lucado has a long history of helping us understand who God is. Now in *Cure for the Common Life* he helps us understand who we are. I hope everyone I know will read it. It's uncommonly good."

> — Mary Graham,
> president of Women of Faith

"Every time I get a chance to hear Max Lucado speak, my life is blessed. Everyone who reads this book will know that they are special in the eyes of God and a very important part of his plan."

> — CeCe Winans,
> gospel music artist

"We all have unique gifts that can be used for God's purposes. Max Lucado's gift is to apply spiritual teachings to our everyday lives, as he has done with *Cure for the Common Life*. Discovering God's unique plan for our lives is both humbling and inspiring: humbling because though we are but a drop in the ocean, the Creator of the universe has a plan for our individual lives, and inspiring, as that plan becomes revealed and our unique talents and attributes get put to work in carrying it out. In understanding the principles Max espouses, you will be inspired to live anything but the common life."

— Rick Perry,
governor of Texas

"Max Lucado has done it again! He has taken simple truths and made them available to all of us. In *Cure for the Common Life* he shows us how to identify and explore our uniqueness and motivates us to put our strengths to work and to live in our sweet spot for the rest of our life."

— Ken Blanchard,
coauthor of *The One-Minute Manager®* and *The Secret*

"To maximize life's potential personally, professionally, and spiritually, you must know the zone in which you are the happiest and most productive. Most people never reach that utopian state because they do not know how to get there. In this book, Max Lucado shows us how to achieve that goal, which he refers to as the 'sweet spot.' I am convinced that by following the detailed guidelines so beautifully written in this book, the reader will be able to find that sweet spot and add new meaning and purpose to life."

— Kenneth H. Cooper,
M.D., M.P.H.

"Max Lucado's *Cure for the Common Life* provides a blueprint for staying above the malaise of quiet, desperate living. With lyrical language, he gives valuable insights for unpacking your uniqueness to glorify God in your eternal vocation. Reading this book will produce in many a 'thank God it's Monday' attitude."

— Barry C. Black,
chaplain of the U.S. Senate

"Other than accepting Christ as Savior, there is no more important discovery for Christians than understanding how God uniquely equips them to work and serve. We are all individually 'wired' by God 'to do good works, which God prepared in advance for us to do.' *Cure for the Common Life* may be the most important book you will ever read if it helps you understand how God equipped you perfectly for service in his kingdom."

— Richard E. Stearns,
president of World Vision U.S.

"I'm so glad for Max Lucado's insightful call for us to live and work as we are intrinsically designed by God."

— Richard J. Foster,
author of *Celebration of Discipline*

"*Cure for the Common Life* is a celebration of the life we have been given and the blessings we have received in great abundance. Refuting the oft-aired charge that Christianity fixates on otherworldly devotion, Max Lucado transforms the everyday into a discovery of self, God, and eternal meaning. In that transformation, this beloved author offers much-needed advice to those who may have sensed a weary emptiness in their daily labors."

— Kenneth W. Starr,
dean of Pepperdine University
School of Law

"Max Lucado has the unusual gift of being able to take God's Word, filter it through human experiences and human circumstances, and have it emerge unscathed and undiluted. The person through whom it passes is transformed by the renewing of his or her mind and heart. In *Cure for the Common Life*, Max and God do it again by showing us how we don't have to be victims of circumstances but can live in a sweeter spot."

— Cal Thomas,
syndicated columnist and host of
After Hours on Fox News channel

"What Jonas Salk did for polio, Max Lucado has done for aimlessness. If you're one of the afflicted masses who feels like you're sliding through life instead of soaring as God intended you, read this book fast! *Cure for the Common Life* is much more than a title—I predict it may be the vaccine that gives life purpose and hope to a whole generation."

— Gene Appel,
teaching pastor of Willow Creek
Community Church and television
commentator

"The message of this book could change your life forever. What if you dared to believe that the God of the universe has made you so unique that without your passionate participation in this life, we would all feel the loss? God waits for us to sing his love song in our own distinct voice."

— Sheila Walsh,
author of *I'm Not Wonder Woman but
God Made Me Wonderful*

"I'm convinced that every single one of us has a 'spiritual DNA' that determines our destiny in this life. Max Lucado calls it our 'sweet spot.' And by reading this terrific new book, you will find yours. It's the right book to read in halftime or anytime."

— Bob Buford,
best-selling author of *Halftime* and
Finishing Well

"Max Lucado's *Cure for the Common Life* leaves you feeling energized, curious to discover your own God-given 'sweet spot.' He encourages you to discover your unique gifts and the specific plan that God has given each of us."

— Dr. Gary Smalley,
author and founder of Smalley
Relationship Center

"Max has once again 'Max-i-mized' my understanding with his sweet-spot style, showing how much better we can be when we're being what God created us to be."

— Pastor Bob Coy,
Calvary Chapel, Fort Lauderdale

"You don't have to read an entire book to write an endorsement for it—unless of course you can't put it down! Such is the case with *Cure for the Common Life*. If your life has become numbingly mundane and you've forgotten that God has a plan for your life, then I suggest you block out a few hours to be reminded of your uniqueness."

— Dave Stone,
Southeast Christian Church,
Louisville, Kentucky

CURE FOR
THE COMMON LIFE

ALSO BY MAX LUCADO

CURE FOR
THE COMMON LIFE

Living in Your Sweet Spot

Max Lucado

THOMAS NELSON
Since 1798

NASHVILLE   DALLAS   MEXICO CITY   RIO DE JANEIRO   BEIJING

Throughout this book are various expressions by Max Lucado related to the SIMA® (System for Identifying Motivated Abilities) technology which have been or are registered as copyrighted under the name of People Management International, Inc. All rights reserved. No part may be reproduced in any form, or by any means, without permission in writing from the publisher.

Published in Nashville, Tennessee, by Thomas Nelson. Thomas Nelson is a registered trademark of Thomas Nelson, Inc.

Thomas Nelson, Inc. titles may be purchased in bulk for educational, business, fund-raising, or sales promotional use. For information, please e-mail SpecialMarkets@ThomasNelson.com.

All Scripture quotations, unless otherwise indicated, are taken from the New King James Version, © 1979, 1980, 1982, Thomas Nelson, Inc., Publishers. Other Scripture references are from the following sources: The Amplified Bible (AMP). Old Testament, © 1965, 1987 by the Zondervan Corporation. The Amplified New Testament, © 1954, 1958, 1987 by the Lockman Foundation. The Contemporary English Version (CEV) © 1991 by the American Bible Society. Used by permission. God's Word (GOD'S WORD) is a copyrighted work of God's Word to the Nations Bible Society. Quotations are used by permission. © 1995 by God's Word to the Nations Bible Society. All rights reserved. The Jerusalem Bible (JB), © 1966, 1967 and 1968 by Darton, Longman & Todd Ltd. and Doubleday. All rights reserved. The Message (MSG), © 1993. Used by permission of NavPress Publishing Group. New American Standard Bible (NASB), © 1960, 1977, 1995 by the Lockman Foundation. The New Century Version® (NCV). © 1987, 1988, 1991 by Thomas Nelson, Inc. All rights reserved. The Holy Bible, New International Version (NIV). © 1973, 1978, 1984, International Bible Society. Used by permission of Zondervan Bible Publishers. The Holy Bible, New Living Translation (NLT), © 1996. Used by permission of Tyndale House Publishers, Inc., Wheaton, Illinois 60189. All rights reserved. J. B. Phillips: The New Testament in Modern English, Revised Edition (PHILLIPS). © J. B. Phillips 1958, 1960, 1972. Used by permission of Macmillan Publishing Co., Inc. The Good News Bible: The Bible in Today's English Version (TEV) © 1976, 1992 by the American Bible Society. The Living Bible (TLB), © 1971 by Tyndale House Publishers, Wheaton, Illinois 60187. All rights reserved. Any italics in the Scripture quotations reflect the author's own emphasis.

ISBN 978-0-8499-2120-9 (Library Edition)

The Library of Congress has cataloged the earlier edition as follows:

Lucado, Max.
    Cure for the common life : living in your sweet spot / Max Lucado.
    p. cm.
    Includes bibliographical references.
    ISBN 978-0-8499-0008-2
    1. Christian life. I. Title.
BV4501.3.L815 2006
248.4—dc22   2005026734

Printed in the United States of America
08 09 10 11 12 LBM 5 4 3 2 1

Denalyn and I gladly dedicate this book
to Doug Kostowski.
Friend, mentor.
Part Merlin, more Arthur.
For a trio of years, we and Miami's moon
saw sprinkles of Camelot.
For the royal moments, we thank you.

This is GOD's Word on the subject: ". . . I know what I'm doing. I have it all planned out—plans to take care of you, not abandon you, plans to give you the future you hope for."

Jeremiah 29:10–11 MSG

CONTENTS

Section Three

Sweet Spot Discovery Guide

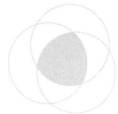

ACKNOWLEDGMENTS

When I was clueless, they had answers; burro headed, they had patience; stuck in dead-end canyons, they brought in a helicopter and pulled me out. What would I do without this chorus of support?

Art Miller and the folks of People Management International Inc. So unselfish with knowledge and generous with time. Because of you, tens of thousands of us better know our purposes and our Maker. Thank you, dear friends.

Rick Wellock. Special appreciation for your efforts in helping me get back on target.

Karen Hill and Liz Heaney. You should open your own line of purses—you sure know how to make them out of the sows' ears I give you. You are the best.

Laura Kendall. The roar you hear is a standing ovation for you and your brilliant career. Congratulations on your retirement. We will miss you!

Carol Bartley. Quietly coming along behind the carpenters, stabilizing the frame with grammar hammers and flubmeters. You amaze me!

Steve and Cheryl Green. God made heaven unending so I'd have enough time to thank you for your loyal and levelheaded friendship.

Susan Perry and Jennifer McKinney. Two earthbound angels who keep our office humming.

Pat Hile and the Oak Hills "My Story" Workshop Team. The way you help people find their story is, in itself, a great story. May God bless your efforts.

Greg and Susan Ligon. Thanks for your vision and oversight of all things Lucado.

The UpWords Staff: Tina Chisholm, Becky Bryant, and Margaret Mechinus. The finest trio on the planet. Thanks for all you do.

The W and Thomas Nelson teams. If publishers had Super Bowls, you'd be a dynasty. Thanks for letting me suit up.

The Oak Hills elders, staff, and church family. An aspen stand of shade on a hot summer day. May thousands find rest in your cover. I do.

John Tafolla. Thanks for sharing your gifts.

My daughters: Jenna, Andrea, and Sara. You've always had better looks than your dad. Now you're smarter than he is. And he couldn't be prouder.

My wife: Denalyn. God sent manna for Moses, fire for Elijah, an angel for Peter, and Denalyn for Max. Miracle doubters need look no further than my wedding album.

And God, my Designer. For writing your story on my life, in spite of my attempts to write my own, I thank you.

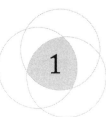

YOUR SWEET SPOT
(YOU HAVE ONE!)

Each person is given something
to do that shows who God is.

1 Corinthians 12:7 MSG

"Sweet spot." Golfers understand the term. So do tennis players. Ever swung a baseball bat or paddled a Ping-Pong ball? If so, you know the oh-so-nice feel of the sweet spot. Connect with these prime inches of real estate and *kapow!* The collective technologies of the universe afterburn the ball into orbit, leaving you Frisbee eyed and strutting. Your arm doesn't tingle, and the ball doesn't ricochet. Your boyfriend remembers birthdays, the tax refund comes early, and the flight attendant bumps you up to first class. Life in the sweet spot rolls like the downhill side of a downwind bike ride.

But you don't have to swing a bat or a club to know this. What engineers give sports equipment, God gave you. A zone, a region, a life precinct in which you were made to dwell. He tailored the curves of your life to fit an empty space in his jigsaw puzzle. And life makes sweet sense when you find your spot. But how do you? Where do you go? What pills do you order, class do you take, or infomercial do you watch? None of the above. Simply quarry . . .

your uniqueness.

Da Vinci painted one *Mona Lisa.* Beethoven composed one Fifth Symphony. And God made one version of you. He custom designed you for a one-of-a-kind assignment. Mine like a gold digger the unique-to-you nuggets from your life.

When I was six years old, my father built us a house. *Architectural Digest* didn't notice, but my mom sure did. Dad constructed it, board by board, every day after work. My youth didn't deter him from giving me a job. He tied an empty nail apron around my waist, placed a magnet in my hands, and sent me on daily patrols around the building site, carrying my magnet only inches off the ground.

One look at my tools and you could guess my job. Stray-nail collector.

One look at yours and the same can be said. Brick by brick, life by life, God is creating a kingdom, a "spiritual house" (1 Pet. 2:5 CEV). He entrusted you with a key task in the project. Examine your tools and discover it. Your ability unveils your destiny. "If anyone ministers, let him do it as *with the ability which God supplies,* that in all things God may be glorified through Jesus Christ" (1 Pet. 4:11). When God gives an assignment, he also gives the skill. Study your skills, then, to reveal your assignment.

Look at you. Your uncanny ease with numbers. Your quenchless curiosity about chemistry. Others stare at blueprints and yawn; you read them and drool. "I was made to do this," you say.

Heed that inner music. No one else hears it the way you do.

At this very moment in another section of the church building in which I write, little kids explore their tools. Preschool classrooms may sound like a cacophony to you and me, but God hears a symphony.

2

A five-year-old sits at a crayon-strewn table. He seldom talks. Classmates have long since set aside their papers, but he ponders his. The colors compel him. He marvels at the gallery of kelly green and navy blue and royal purple. Masterpiece in hand, he'll race to Mom and Dad, eager to show them his kindergarten Picasso.

> God endows us with gifts so we can make him known.

His sister, however, forgets her drawing. She won't consume the home commute with tales of painted pictures. She'll tell tales of tales. "The teacher told us a new story today!" And the girl will need no prodding to repeat it.

Another boy cares less about the story and the drawings and more about the other kids. He spends the day wearing a "Hey, listen to me!" expression, lingering at the front of the class, testing the patience of the teacher. He relishes attention, evokes reactions. His theme seems to be "Do it this way. Come with me. Let's try this."

Meaningless activities at an insignificant age? Or subtle hints of hidden strengths? I opt for the latter. The quiet boy with the color fascination may someday brighten city walls with murals. His sister may pen a screenplay or teach literature to curious coeds. And the kid who recruits followers today might eventually do the same on behalf of a product, the poor, or even his church.

What about you? Our Maker gives assignments to people, "to each according to each one's unique ability" (Matt. 25:15).[1] As he calls, he equips. Look back over your life. What have you consistently done well? What have you loved to do? Stand at the intersection of your affections and successes and find your uniqueness.

You have one. A divine spark.[2] An uncommon call to an uncommon life. "The Spirit has given each of us a *special way* of serving others" (1 Cor. 12:7 CEV). So much for the excuse "I don't have anything to offer." Did the apostle Paul say, "The Spirit has given *some* of us . . ."? Or, "The Spirit has given *a few* of us . . ."? No. "The Spirit has given *each of us* a special way of serving others." Enough of this self-deprecating "I can't do anything."

And enough of its arrogant opposite: "I have to do everything." No, you don't! You're not God's solution to society, but a solution in society. Imitate Paul, who said, "Our goal is to stay within the boundaries of God's plan for us" (2 Cor. 10:13 NLT). Clarify your contribution.

Don't worry about skills you don't have. Don't covet strengths others do have. Just extract your uniqueness. "Kindle afresh the gift of God which is in you" (2 Tim. 1:6 NASB). And do so to . . .

make a big deal out of God.

"Everything comes from God alone. Everything lives by his power, and everything is for his glory" (Rom. 11:36 TLB). The breath you just took? God gave that. The blood that just pulsed through your heart? Credit God. The light by which you read and the brain with which you process? He gave both.

Everything comes from him . . . and exists for him. We exist to exhibit God, to display his glory. We serve as canvases for his brush stroke, papers for his pen, soil for his seeds, glimpses of his image.

Stand at the intersection of your affections and successes and find your uniqueness.

Texas A&M's T-shirted football fans model our role. In the aftermath of September 11, many Americans sought an opportunity to demonstrate patriotism and solidarity. Five students set the pace. They designated the next home football game as Red, White, and Blue Out and sold T-shirts to each of the seventy thousand fans. Kyle Field morphed into a human flag as those seated in the third deck wore red, the second deck wore white, and the lower deck wore blue. Newspapers across America splashed the picture on front pages.³

Newsworthy indeed! How often do thousands of people billboard a singular, powerful message? God fashioned us to do so for him. "Each person is given something to do that shows who God is" (1 Cor. 12:7 MSG). He distributes, not shirts, but strengths. He sends people, not to bleacher seats, but to life assignments: "Go to your place. Dispatch your abilities, and unfurl my goodness."

Most refuse. Few cooperate. We accept the present, but neglect its purpose. We accept the gift, thank you, but ignore the Giver and promote self. Why, some of us have been known to parade up and down the aisles, shouting, "Hey, look at me!"

Need an explanation for the anarchy in the world? You just read it. When you center-stage your gifts and I pump my image and no one gives a lick about honoring God, dare we expect anything short of chaos?

God endows us with gifts so we can make him known. Period. God endues the Olympian with speed, the salesman with savvy, the surgeon with skill. Why? For gold medals, closed sales, or healed bodies? Only partially.

The big answer is to make a big to-do out of God. Brandish him. Herald him. "God has given gifts to each of you from his great variety of spiritual gifts. Manage them well. . . . *Then God will be given glory*" (1 Pet. 4:10–11 NLT).

Live so that "he'll get all the credit as the One mighty in everything— encores to the end of time. Oh, yes!" (1 Pet. 4:11 MSG). Exhibit God with your uniqueness. When you magnify your Maker with your strengths, when your contribution enriches God's reputation, your days grow suddenly sweet. And to really dulcify your world, use your uniqueness to make a big deal about God . . .

every day of your life.

Heaven's calendar has seven Sundays a week. God sanctifies each day. He conducts holy business at all hours and in all places. He uncommons the common by turning kitchen sinks into shrines, cafés into convents, and nine-to-five workdays into spiritual adventures.

Workdays? Yes, workdays. He ordained your work as something good. Before he gave Adam a wife or a child, even before he gave Adam britches, God gave Adam a job. "Then the LORD God took the man and put him into the garden of Eden to cultivate it and keep it" (Gen. 2:15 NASB). Innocence, not indolence, characterized the first family.

God views work worthy of its own engraved commandment: "You shall work six days, but on the seventh day you shall rest" (Exod. 34:21 NASB). We like the second half of that verse. But emphasis on the

> Your ability unveils your destiny.

day of rest might cause us to miss the command to work: "You *shall* work six days." Whether you work at home or in the marketplace, your work matters to God.

And your work matters to society. We need you! Cities need plumbers. Nations need soldiers. Stoplights break. Bones break. We need people to repair the first and set the second. Someone has to raise kids, raise cane, and manage the kids who raise Cain.

Whether you log on or lace up for the day, you imitate God. Jehovah himself worked for the first six days of creation. Jesus said, "My Father never stops working, and so I keep working, too" (John 5:17 NCV). Your career consumes half of your lifetime. Shouldn't it broadcast God? Don't those forty to sixty hours a week belong to him as well?

The Bible never promotes workaholism or an addiction to employment as pain medication. But God unilaterally calls all the physically able to till the gardens he gives. God honors work. So honor God in your work.

"There is nothing better for a man than to eat and drink and tell himself that his labor is good" (Eccles. 2:24 NASB).

I just heard a groan.

"But, Max," someone objects, "my work is simply that—work! It pays my bills, but numbs my soul." (You're only a few pages from some help.)

"Job satisfaction? How about job survival? How do I survive a job misfit?" (I have some ideas.)

"I have no clue how to find my skill." (By the end of the book you will.)

"Honor God? After the mess I've made of my life?" (Don't miss the chapter on mercy.)

For now, here is the big idea:

Use your uniqueness (what you do)
to make a big deal out of God (why you do it)
every day of your life (where you do it).

At the convergence of all three, you'll find the cure for the common life: your sweet spot.

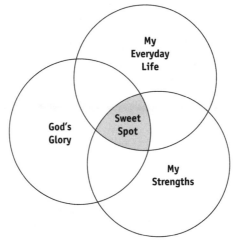

Sweet spot. You have one, you know. Your life has a plot; your years have a theme. You can do something in a manner that no one else can. And when you find it and do it, another sweet spot is discovered. Let's find yours.

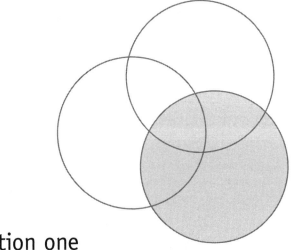

section one

USE YOUR UNIQUENESS

to make a big deal out of God
every day of your life

Endless cotton crops had sucked the nutrients out of Southern soil. Post–Civil War farmers faced scorched land and scrawny crops. George Washington Carver, a professor at Alabama's Tuskegee Institute, offered a solution. Change crops and restore nitrogen and fertility to the soil. Grow sweet potatoes, cowpeas, soybeans, and, most of all, peanuts. But Carver couldn't convince the farmers.

It took a boll weevil to do that.

Out of Mexico they swarmed, through Texas, into Louisiana and Mississippi. By 1915 the cotton-consuming bug had reached Alabama. Carver saw the plague as an opportunity. "Burn off your infested cotton," he pleaded, "and plant peanuts."

But who would buy them?

An elderly widow knocked on Carver's door. After planting and harvesting peanuts, she had hundreds of pounds left over. She was not alone. Carver discovered barns and storehouses piled high with peanuts. They were rotting in the fields for lack of a market.

Years later he recalled how he retreated to his favorite spot in the woods, seeking God's wisdom.

"Oh, Mister Creator," he cried out, "why did you make this universe?"

And the Creator answered, "You want to know too much for that little mind of yours. Ask me something more your size."

So I said, "Dear Mister Creator, tell me what man was made for."

Again He spoke to me and said, "Little man, you are still asking for more than you can handle. Cut down the extent of your request and improve the intent."

Then I asked my last question. "Mister Creator, why did you make the peanut?"

"That's better," the Lord said.

And he gave me a handful of peanuts and went back with me to the laboratory, and together we got down to work.[1]

Working day and night, Carver tore apart the peanut and unlocked the chemical magic that would turn loss into profit. In less than five years, peanut production turned his Alabama county into one of the wealthiest sections of the state. During his lifetime, Carver extracted more than three hundred products from the peanut.

This section is about your finding your peanut—the tailor-made task that honors God, helps others, and thrills you.

2

UNPACK YOUR BAG

He has filled them with skill.

Exodus 35:35 JB

You were born prepacked. God looked at your entire life, determined your assignment, and gave you the tools to do the job.

Before traveling, you do something similar. You consider the demands of the journey and pack accordingly. Cold weather? Bring a jacket. Business meeting? Carry the laptop. Time with grandchildren? Better take some sneakers and pain medication.

God did the same with you. *Joe will research animals . . . install curiosity. Meagan will lead a private school . . . add an extra dose of management. I need Eric to comfort the sick . . . include a healthy share of compassion. Denalyn will marry Max . . . instill a double portion of patience.*

"Each of us is an original" (Gal. 5:26 MSG). God packed you on purpose for a purpose. Is this news to you? If so, you may be living out of the wrong bag.

I once grabbed the wrong bag at the airport. The luggage looked like mine. Same size. Same material. Same color. Thrilled that it had emerged early from the baggage catacombs, I yanked it off the carousel and headed to the hotel. One glance inside, however, and I knew I'd made a mistake.

13

Wrong size, style, and gender. (Besides, my pants would be too short with stiletto heels.)

What would you do in such a case? You could make do with what you have. Cram your body into the tight clothes, deck out in other-gender jewelry, and head out for your appointments. But would you? Only at risk of job loss and jail time.

No, you'd hunt down your own bag. Issue an all-points bulletin. Call the airport. Call the airlines. The taxi service. The FBI. Hire bloodhounds and private investigators. You'd try every possible way to find the person who can't find her suitcase and is wondering what gooney bird failed to check the nametag.

No one wants to live out of someone else's bag.

Then why do we? Odds are, someone has urged a force fit into clothes not packed for you.

Parents do. The dad puts an arm around his young son. "Your great-granddad was a farmer. Your granddad was a farmer. I'm a farmer. And you, my son, will someday inherit the farm."

A teacher might. She warns the young girl who wants to be a stay-at-home mom, "Don't squander your skills. With your gifts you could make it to the top. The professional world is the way to go."

God packed you on purpose for a purpose.

Church leaders assign luggage from the pulpit. "God seeks world-changing, globetrotting missionaries. Jesus was a missionary. Do you want to please your Maker? Follow him into the holy vocation. Spend your life on foreign soil."

Sound counsel or poor advice? That depends on what God packed in the person's bag.

A bequeathed farm blesses the individualist and physically active. But what if God fashioned the farmer's son with a passion for literature or medicine?

Work outside the home might be a great choice for some, but what if God gave the girl a singular passion for kids and homemaking?

Those wired to learn languages and blaze trails should listen up to sermons promoting missionary service. But if foreign cultures frustrate you while predictability invigorates you, would you be happy as a missionary?

No, but you would contribute to these mind-numbing statistics:

- Unhappiness on the job affects one-fourth of the American work force.[1]

- One-fourth of employees view their jobs as the number one stressor in their lives.[2]

- Seven out of ten people are neither motivated nor competent to perform the basics of their job.[3]

- Forty-three percent of employees feel anger toward their employers often or very often as a result of feeling overworked.[4]

Feel the force of these figures. You wonder why workbound commuters seem so cranky? "Fully 70 percent of us go to work without much enthusiasm or passion."[5] Most wage earners spend forty of their eighty waking weekday hours trudging through the streets of Dullsville.

Such misery can't help but sour families, populate bars, and pay the salaries of therapists. If 70 percent of us dread Mondays, dream of Fridays, and slug through the rest of the week, won't our relationships suffer? Won't our work suffer? Won't our health suffer? One study states, "Problems at work are more strongly associated with health complaints than any other life stressor—more so than even financial problems or family problems."[6]

Such numbers qualify as an epidemic. An epidemic of commonness.

Someone sucked the sparkle out of our days. A stale fog has settled over our society. Week after week of energy-sapping sameness. Walls painted gray with routine. Commuters dragging their dread to the office. Buildings packed with people working to live rather than living to work. Boredom. Mediocre performance.

The cure? God's prescription begins with unpacking your bags. You exited the womb uniquely equipped. David states it this way: "My frame was not hidden from you when I was made in the secret place. When I was woven together in the depths of the earth, your eyes saw my unformed body. All the days ordained for me were written in your book before one of them came to be" (Ps. 139:15–16 NIV).

> You cannot be anything you want to be.
> But you can be everything God wants you to be.

Spelunk these verses with me. David emphasizes the pronoun "you" as if to say "you, God, and you alone." "The secret place" suggests a hidden and safe place, concealed from intruders and evil. Just as an artist takes a canvas into a locked studio, so God took you into his hidden chamber where you were "woven together." Moses used the same word to describe the needlework of the tabernacle's inner curtains—stitched together by skillful hands for the highest purpose (see Exod. 26:1; 36:8; 38:9). The Master Weaver selected your temperament threads, your character texture, the yarn of your personality—all before you were born. God did not drop you into the world utterly defenseless and empty-handed. You arrived fully equipped. "All the days ordained . . ." Day of birth and day of death. Days of difficulty and victory. What motivates you, what exhausts you . . . God authored—and authors—it all.

Other translations employ equally intriguing verbs:

You . . . knit me together. (v. 13 NLT)

I was woven together in the dark of the womb. (v. 15 NLT)

I was . . . intricately and curiously wrought [as if embroidered with various colors]. (v. 15 AMP)

My hands have never embroidered a stitch, but my mom's have. In pre-dishwasher days when mothers drafted young sons into kitchen duty to dry dishes, I grew too acquainted with her set of embroidered dishtowels. She had embellished sturdy white cloths with colorful threads: seven towels, each bearing the name of a different day. Her artisan skills rendered common towels uncommonly unique.

God did the same with you! How would you answer this multiple-choice question?

I am

_____ a coincidental collision of particles.

_____ an accidental evolution of molecules.

_____ soulless flotsam in the universe.

_____ "fearfully and wonderfully made" (v. 14), "skillfully wrought" (v. 15).

Don't dull your life by missing this point: You are more than statistical chance, more than a marriage of heredity and society, more than a conflu-ence of inherited chromosomes and childhood trauma. More than a walk-ing weather vane whipped about by the cold winds of fate. Thanks to God, you have been "sculpted from nothing into something" (v. 15 MSG).

Envision Rodin carving *The Thinker* out of a rock. The sculptor chisels away a chunk of stone, shapes the curve of a kneecap, sands the forehead . . .

Now envision God doing the same: sculpting the way you are before you even were, engraving you with

an eye for organization,

an ear for fine music,

a heart that beats for justice and fairness,

a mind that understands quantum physics,

the tender fingers of a caregiver, or

the strong legs of a runner.

He made you *you-nique.*

Secular thinking, as a whole, doesn't buy this. Secular society sees no author behind the book, no architect behind the house, no purpose behind or beyond life. Society sees no bag and certainly never urges you to unpack one. It simply says, "You can be anything you want to be."

Be a butcher if you want to, a sales rep if you like. Be an ambassador if you really care. You can be anything you want to be. If you work hard enough. But can you? If God didn't pack within you the meat sense of a butcher, the people skills of a salesperson, or the world vision of an ambassador, can you be one? An unhappy, dissatisfied one perhaps. But a fulfilled one? No. Can an acorn become a rose, a whale fly like a bird, or lead become gold? Absolutely not. You cannot be anything you want to be. But you can be everything God wants you to be.

Søren Kierkegaard echoed the teaching of Scripture when he wrote, "At each man's birth there comes into being an eternal vocation for him, expressly for him. To be true to himself in relation to this eternal vocation is the highest thing a man can practice."[7]

God never prefabs or mass-produces people. No slapdash shaping. "I make all things new," he declares (Rev. 21:5). He didn't hand you your granddad's bag or your aunt's life; he personally and deliberately packed you.

When you live out of the bag God gave, you discover an uncommon joy. Haven't you seen examples of this?

I recently flew to St. Louis on a commercial airline. The attendant was so grumpy I thought she'd had lemons for breakfast. She made her instructions clear: sit down, buckle up, and shut up! I dared not request anything lest she push the eject button.

Perhaps I caught her on the wrong day, or maybe she caught herself in the wrong career.

Two weeks later I took another flight. This attendant had been imported from heaven. She introduced herself to each passenger, had us greet each other, and then sang a song over the intercom! I had to ask her, "Do you like your work?"

"I love it!" she beamed. "For years I taught elementary school and relished each day. But then they promoted me. I went from a class of kids to an office of papers. Miserable! I resigned, took some months to study myself, found this opportunity, and snagged it. Now I can't wait to come to work!"

> You can do something no one else can do in a fashion no one else can do it.

Too few people can say what she said. Few people do what she did. One job-placement firm suggests only 1 percent of its clients have made a serious study of their skills.[8]

Don't imitate their mistake. "Don't live carelessly, unthinkingly. Make sure you understand what the Master wants" (Eph. 5:17 MSG). You can do something no one else can do in a fashion no one else can do it. Exploring and extracting your uniqueness excites you, honors God, and expands his kingdom. So "make a careful exploration of who you are and the work you have been given, and then sink yourself into that" (Gal. 6:4 MSG).

Discover and deploy your knacks.

Charlie Steinmetz did. He designed the generators that powered Henry

Ford's first assembly lines in Dearborn, Michigan. Sometime after he retired, the generators stalled out, bringing the entire plant to a halt. Ford's engineers couldn't find the problem, so he called his old friend Charlie. Steinmetz fiddled with this gauge, jiggled that lever, tried this button, played with a few wires, and after a few hours threw the master switch. The motors kicked on, and the system returned to normal. Some days later Ford received a bill from Steinmetz for $10,000. Ford found the charge excessive and wrote his friend a note: "Charlie: It seems awfully steep, this $10,000, for a man who for just a little while tinkered around with a few motors." Steinmetz wrote a new bill and sent it back to Mr. Ford. "Henry: For tinkering around with motors, $10; for knowing where to tinker, $9,990."[9]

You tinker unlike anyone else. Explore and extract your tinker talent. A gift far greater than $10,000 awaits you. "Remember that the Lord will give a reward to everyone . . . for doing good" (Eph. 6:8 NCV).

When you do the most what you do the best, you put a smile on God's face. What could be better than that?

READ YOUR
LIFE BACKWARD

God is working in you to help you want to do
and be able to do what pleases him.

Philippians 2:13 NCV

Every so often we find ourselves riding the flow of life. Not resisting or thrashing it, but just riding it. A stronger current lifts, channels, and carries, daring us to declare, "I was made to do this."

Do you know the flow? Sure you do.

Go back into your youth. What activity lured you off the gray sidewalk of sameness into an amusement park of sights, sounds, and colors? Oh, the fireworks. Every nerve ending buzzed; every brain cell sizzled; all five senses kicked in.

What were you doing? Assembling a model airplane in the garage? Helping your aunt plant seeds in the garden? Organizing games for your playground buddies? To this day you can remember the details of those days: the smell of cement glue, the feel of moist dirt, the squeals of excited kids. Magical. The only bad moment was the final moment.

Fast-forward a few years. Let childhood become adolescence, elementary

21

school become middle school, then high school. Reflect on favorite memories: those full-flight moments of unclocked time and unlocked energy. All cylinders clicking. Again, what were you doing? What entranced you? Energized you? Engaged you?

If age and patience allow, indulge in one more pondering. Analyze your best days as a young adult. No upstream flailing. No battling against the current. During the times you rode the tide, what activities carried you? What objects did you hold? What topics did you consider?

Do you note common themes? To be sure, the scenery changes, and characters drop out. The details may alter, but your bent, your passion, what you yearn to do, you keep doing. The current of life's river keeps dropping you at a particular bank.

Always

> fixing things,
> challenging systems,
> organizing facts,
> championing the small,
> networking behind the scenes, or
> seeking center stage.

Always doing the same thing.

And why not? It comes easily to you. Not without struggle, but with less struggle than your peers. You wondered why others found hitting a baseball or diagraming a sentence so difficult. Anyone can assemble a television from a do-it-yourself kit, right?

Wrong. But David could. At the age of twelve, he did. He began the project with his dad. And when the navy called his father out to sea, David stayed at it. He spent after-school hours tracing diagrams, installing tubes, and soldering wires. By the time his father returned, the family had a new television.

To this day, a quarter of a century later, David's eyes still dance when he describes the moment the first image appeared on the screen. No surprise that he earned a degree in civil engineering. David loves to put stuff together.

He still does. Just ask the one hundred or so kids who attend Carver Academy, a state-of-the-art inner-city school in San Antonio. David Robinson built it. Yes, he played MVP-level basketball, but he also builds things. If the past is a teacher, he always will.

"The child is father of the man," wrote William Wordsworth.[1] Want direction for the future? Then read your life backward.

Our past presents our future.

Job-placement consultants at People Management International Inc. have asked over seventy thousand clients this question: what things have you done in life that you enjoyed doing and believe you did well? "In every case," writes founder Arthur Miller Jr., "the data showed that people had invariably reverted to the same pattern of functioning whenever they had done something they enjoyed doing and did well."[2]

Or, to put it succinctly, our past presents our future. Can this be true? Can childhood interests forecast adult abilities? Can early leanings serve as first sketches of the final portrait?

Biographies of spiritual heroes suggest so. Start with the Egyptian prince. As a young man he excelled in the ways of the court. He mastered the laws of the ancient land. He studied at the feet of the world's finest astronomers, mathematicians, and lawyers. Fifteen hundred years later he was remembered as "learned in all the wisdom of the Egyptians, and . . . mighty in words and deeds" (Acts 7:22).

What little we know of Moses's upbringing tells us this: he displayed an affinity for higher learning and an allergy to injustice. Remember his first adult appearance in Scripture? He saw an Egyptian beating a Hebrew slave and killed the Egyptian. The next day Moses saw two Hebrews fighting and intervened again. This time one of the Hebrews asked, "Who made you a prince and a judge over us?" (Exod. 2:14).

A prince and a judge. How accurate is the description? Turn to the second act. To avoid arrest, Moses scampered into the badlands, where he encountered more injustice. "Now the priest of Midian had seven daughters. And they came and drew water, and they filled the troughs to water their father's flock. Then the shepherds came and drove them away; but Moses stood up and helped them, and watered their flock" (Exod. 2:16–17).

What drove Moses to protect these young women? Their beauty? His thirst? Maybe both or maybe more. Maybe irrepressible seeds of fairness grew in his soul. When he decked a cruel Egyptian or scattered chauvinistic shepherds, was he acting out his God-given bent toward justice?

The rest of his life would say so. Forty years after he fled Egypt, Moses returned, this time with God's burning-bush blessing and power. He dismantled Pharaoh and unshackled the Hebrews. Moses *the prince* escorted his people into a new kingdom. Moses *the judge* framed the Torah and midwifed the Hebrew law.

The strengths of his youth unveiled the passions of his life.

> God planned and packed you on purpose for his purpose.

Fast-forward nearly two millenniums and consider another case. Like Moses, this young scholar displayed a youthful love of the law. He studied at the feet of Jerusalem's finest teachers. He followed the Torah with razor-sharp precision. He aligned himself with the Pharisees, ardent observers of Scripture. They defended the law with zeal. And "zeal" is the term he used to describe his youth. "Zealous?" he wrote. "Yes, in fact, I harshly persecuted the church" (Phil. 3:6 NLT).

Young Saul's ardor prompted his initial appearance in Scripture. Just like Moses, a murder brought him to the stage. Angry members of the

Jewish council "cast [Stephen] out of the city and stoned him. And the witnesses laid down their clothes at the feet of a young man named Saul" (Acts 7:58).

Call Saul misguided, misled, or mistaken—but don't call Saul mild. If you scratched him, he bled commitment. Whether he was Saul, the legalist, or Paul, the apostle of grace, he couldn't sit still. Cause driven. Single-minded. Focused like a hawk on prey. Peter might tolerate the hypocrisy of the church. Not Paul. With him, you were either in or out, cold or hot. Whether persecuting disciples or making them, Paul impacted people.

An early strength forecast his lifelong trait.

Have time for one more example?

Consider the younger days of Billy Frank, the elder son of a dairy farmer. His dad rousted him out of bed around two thirty each morning to perform chores. Younger brother Melvin relished the work, tagging along at his father's side, eager to take his turn long before he was able.

Not Billy Frank. He and Melvin had the same father, but not the same bent. The minute he finished his chores, Billy Frank dashed into the hayloft with a copy of *Tarzan* or *Marco Polo*. By the age of fourteen, he had traced *The Decline and Fall of the Roman Empire*. Missionary stories, accounts of brave servants in faraway lands, fascinated the boy most of all.

Later, as a college student at Florida Bible Institute, he visited with every evangelist who gave him time. He served their tables, polished their shoes, caddied for them, carried their luggage, posed to have his picture taken with them, and wrote home to tell his mother how much he "longed to be like this one or that one."[3]

Billy Frank bore one more trademark: energy. His mother remembered, "There was never any quietness about Billy. . . . I was relieved when he started school." He was hyperactive before the term existed. Always running, inquiring, questioning. "He never wears down," his parents told the doctor. "It's just the way he's built," the doctor assured.[4]

Study Billy Frank's mosaic: fascinated with books and words, intrigued by missionaries and faraway lands, blessed with boundless energy . . . What happens with a boy like that?

And what happens when God's Spirit convinces him of sin and salvation? Young Billy Frank decided to drop his middle name and go by his first. After all, an evangelist needs to be taken seriously. And people took Billy Frank Graham very seriously.

What if Graham had ignored his heart? What if his parents had forced him to stay on the farm? What if no one had noticed God's pattern in his life?

> The oak indwells the acorn.

What if you fail to notice yours?

Remember, God planned and packed you on purpose for his purpose. "It is God himself who has made us what we are and given us new lives from Christ Jesus; and long ages ago he planned that we should spend these lives in helping others" (Eph. 2:10 TLB).

You are heaven's custom design. God "formed you in your mother's body" (Isa. 44:2 NCV). He determined your every detail. "Who made a person's mouth? And who makes someone deaf . . . ? Or who gives a person sight or blindness? It is I, the LORD" (Exod. 4:11 NCV).

At a moment before moments existed, the sovereign Star Maker resolved, "I will make _____." Your name goes in the blank. Then he continued with, "And I will make him/her _____ and _____ and _____ and _____." Fill those blanks with your characteristics. Insightful. Clever. Detail oriented. Restless. And since you are God's idea, you are a good idea. What God said about Jeremiah, he said about you: "Before I made you in your mother's womb, I chose you. Before you were born, I set you apart for a special work" (Jer. 1:5 NCV).

Set apart for a special work.

During a college break I made extra money by sweeping metal shavings.

Several dozen machinists spent ten hours a day shaping steel at their lathes. Need a six-inch square of quarter-inch sheet metal? They could cut it. Need screw holes in the hinge? They could bore them. Need a thin-stripped tin? Just tell the machinist. The workers shaped the steel according to its purpose. God does the same.

He shaped you according to yours. How else can you explain yourself? Your ability to diagnose an engine problem by the noise it makes, to bake a cake without a recipe. You knew the Civil War better than your American history teacher. You know the name of every child in the orphanage. How do you explain such quirks of skill?

His design defines your destiny.

God. He knew young Israel would need a code, so he gave Moses a love for the law. He knew the doctrine of grace would need a fiery advocate, so he set Paul ablaze. And in your case, he knew what your generation would need and gave it. He designed you. And *his design defines your destiny.* Remember Peter's admonition? "If anyone ministers, let him do it as with the ability which God supplies" (1 Pet. 4:11).

I encountered walking proof of this truth on a trip to Central America. Dave,[5] a fellow American, was celebrating his sixty-first birthday with friends at the language school where my daughter was studying Spanish. My question—"What brings you here?"—opened a biographical flood-gate. Drugs, sex, divorce, jail—Dave's first four decades read like a gangster's diary. But then God called him. Just as God called Moses, Paul, and millions, God called Dave.

His explanation went something like this. "I've always been able to fix things. All my life when stuff broke, people called me. A friend told me about poor children in Central America, so I came up with an idea. I find homes with no fathers and no plumbing. I install sinks and toilets and love kids. That's what I do. That's what I was made to do."

Sounds like Dave has found the cure for the common life. He's living in his sweet spot. What about you? What have you always done well? And what have you always loved to do?

That last question trips up a lot of well-meaning folks. *God wouldn't let me do what I like to do—would he?* According to Paul, he would. "God is working in you to help you *want to do* and *be able to do* what pleases him" (Phil. 2:13 NCV). Your Designer couples the "want to" with the "be able to." Desire shares the driver's seat with ability. "Delight yourself in the LORD and he will give you the desires of your heart" (Ps. 37:4 NIV). Your Father is too gracious to assign you to a life of misery. As Thomas Aquinas wrote, "Human life would seem to consist in that in which each man most delights, that for which he especially strives, and that which he particularly wishes to share with his friends."[6]

I recently met a twenty-year-old who needed to hear this. Just discharged from the military, he was pondering his future. He bore a square jaw, a forearm tattoo, and a common question. He didn't know what to do with the rest of his life. As we shared a flight, he told me about his uncle, a New England priest. "What a great man," the ex-soldier sighed. "He helps kids and feeds the hungry. I'd love to make a difference like that."

So I asked him the question of this chapter. "What were some occasions when you did something you love to do and did it well?"

He dismissed me at first. "Aw, what I love to do is stupid."

"Try me," I invited.

"Well, I love to rebuild stuff."

"What do you mean?"

He spoke of an old coffee table he had found in a garage. Seeing its potential, he shaved off the paint, fixed the broken legs, and restored it. With great pride, he presented it to his mom.

"Tell me another time," I prompted.

"This one is really dumb," he discounted. "But when I worked at a butcher shop, I used to find meat on the bones others threw out. My boss loved me! I could find several pounds of product just by giving the bone a second try."

As the plane was nosing down, I tested a possibility with him. "You love to salvage stuff. You salvage furniture, salvage meat. God gave you the ability to find a treasure in someone else's trash."

My idea surprised him. "God? God did that?"

"Yes, God. Your ability to restore a table is every bit as holy as your uncle's ability to restore a life." You would have thought he'd just been handed a newborn baby. As my words sank in, the tough soldier teared up.

See your desires as gifts to heed rather than longings to suppress, and you'll feel the same joy.

So go ahead; reflect on your life. What have you always done well and loved to do?

Some find such a question too simple. Don't we need to measure something?[7] Aptitude or temperament? We consult teachers and tea leaves, read manuals and horoscopes. We inventory spiritual gifts[8] and ancestors. While some of these strategies might aid us, a simpler answer lies before us. Or, better stated, lies within us.

The oak indwells the acorn. Read your life backward and check your supplies. Rerelish your moments of success and satisfaction. For in the merger of the two, you find your uniqueness.

4

STUDY YOUR
S.T.O.R.Y.

The LORD looks from heaven;
He sees all the sons of men. . . .
He fashions their hearts individually;
He considers all their works.

Psalm 33:13, 15

Consider this idea for a reality television show. The goal is simple. Each contestant must journey to a certain city, find a prescribed neighborhood, and assume a particular role. Call it *Find Your Place.*[1]

The fly in the ointment? No one tells you where to go or what to do when you get there. The host identifies no city. He designates no countries. He distributes no job descriptions. All contestants must discern their destinations by virtue of one tool. Their supplies. Upon leaving the starting spot, each one is handed a bag of supplies that provide the clues to that person's destination.

The host, for example, hands one person a cowhide bag crammed with sweaters, a parka, and a soccer ball. In the side pocket, the contestant finds coins. Argentine currency. A teacher's attendance sheet from a language school. Looks like the destination and position are shaping up.

Another is given diving equipment. Oxygen tanks. Fins and goggles. Someone is going near an ocean. And what's this? A wrench? Deep-sea divers don't carry tools. Wait, here is yet another clue. A book. Diagrams of offshore drilling rigs. This person seems to be headed to a drilling platform.

Networks won't syndicate the show, you say? Too boring? Take your concern to the originator of the plot. God. He developed the story line and enlisted you as a participant.

You didn't exit the womb with your intended career tattooed on your chest. No printout of innate skills accompanied your birth. But as life progressed, you began noticing your gifts. Skills, revealed. Knacks, uncovered.

God gave those. "It is God himself who has made us what we are and given us new lives from Christ Jesus; and long ages ago he planned that we should spend these lives in helping others" (Eph. 2:10 TLB).

The cure for commonness begins with strength extraction. No one else has your skill makeup. Disregard it at your peril. An oil-rig repairman won't feel at home in an Argentine schoolroom. And if God made you to teach Argentine kids, you won't enjoy offshore derrick repair. And the kids in the class and the workers on the platform? Don't they want the right person in the right place? Indeed, they do. You do too. And, most of all, God does. You are the only you he made.

In their book *Behavioral Genetics,* a team of scientists declare:

You are the only you God made.

> Each of us has the capacity to generate 10^{3000} eggs or sperm with unique sets of genes. If we consider 10^{3000} possible eggs being generated by an individual woman and the same number of sperm being generated by an individual man, the likelihood of anyone else with your set of genes in the past or in the future becomes infinitesimal.[2]

If numbers numb you, let me simplify. God made you and broke the mold. "The LORD looks from heaven; He sees all the sons of men. From the place of His dwelling He looks on all the inhabitants of the earth; *He fashions their hearts individually;* He considers all their works" (Ps. 33:13–15). Every single baby is a brand-new idea from the mind of God.

Scan history for your replica; you won't find it. God tailor-made you. He "personally formed and made each one" (Isa. 43:7 MSG). No box of "backup yous" sits in God's workshop. You aren't one of many bricks in the mason's pile or one of a dozen bolts in the mechanic's drawer. You are it! And if you aren't you, we don't get you. The world misses out.

You are heaven's Halley's comet; we have one shot at seeing you shine. You offer a gift to society that no one else brings. If you don't bring it, it won't be brought.

Consider a wacky example of this truth. I jogged through my neighborhood the other day under a cloud. Not a cloud of rain, but a cloud of self-doubt. The challenges of life seemed to outnumber the resources, and I questioned my ability. And, quite frankly, I questioned God's wisdom. *Are you sure I'm the right man for this job?* was the theme of my prayer.

Apparently God really wanted to give me an answer, because I heard one. From on high. From a deep, booming voice. "You're doing a good job!" I stopped dead in my Reeboks and looked up. Seeing nothing in the clouds, I shifted my attention to the roof of a house. There he waved at me—a painter dressed in white and leaning against a dormer. I waved back. And I wondered and almost asked, "How did you know I needed to hear that?"

Did I have a brush with an angel? Did I see an angel with a brush? Was the worker sunstruck? This much I know. A painter spots a middle-aged guy with a bald spot puffing through the streets and thinks, *The guy could use a good word.* So he gives it. "You're doing a good job!"

Am I stretching theology a bit when I suggest that God put the man there, at least in part, for me? Long before time had time, God saw each moment in time, including that one. He saw a minister in need of a word. He saw a fellow with a skill for painting and a heart for encouragement. He put one on the street and the other on the roof so the second could encourage the first. Multiply that tiny event by billions, and behold the way God sustains his world. "God, who makes everything work together, will work you into his most excellent harmonies" (Phil. 4:9 MSG).

The Unseen Conductor prompts this orchestra we call living. When gifted teachers aid struggling students and skilled managers disentangle bureaucratic knots, when dog lovers love dogs and number-crunchers zero balance the account, when you and I do the most what we do the best for the glory of God, we are "marvelously functioning parts in Christ's body" (Rom. 12:5 MSG).

You play no small part, because there is no small part to be played. "All of you together are Christ's body, and each one of you is a separate and necessary part of it" (1 Cor. 12:27 NLT). "Separate" and "necessary." Unique and essential. No one else has been given your lines. God "shaped each person in turn" (Ps. 33:15 MSG). The Author of the human drama entrusted your part to you alone. Live your life, or it won't be lived. We need you to be you.

You need you to be you.

You can't be your hero, your parent, or your big brother. You might imitate their golf swing or hair style, but you can't be them. You can only be you. All you have to give is what you've been given to give. Concentrate on who you are and what you have. "Don't compare yourself with others. Each of you must take responsibility for doing the creative best you can with your own life" (Gal. 6:4–5 MSG).

Before Thomas Merton followed Christ, he followed money, fame, and society. He shocked many when he exchanged it all for the life of a Trappist monk in a Kentucky monastery. Business-world colleagues speculated what he must have become. They envisioned a silenced, suffering version of their friend dutifully sludging through a life of penance. After thirteen years, a colleague, Mark van Doren, visited him and then reported back to the others: "He looked a little older; but as we sat and talked I could see no important difference in him, and once I interrupted a reminiscence of his by laughing. 'Tom,' I said, 'you haven't changed at all.' 'Why should I? Here,' he said, 'our duty is to be more ourselves, not less.'"[3]

> If you aren't you, we don't get you. The world misses out.

God never called you to be anyone other than you. But he does call on you to be the best *you* you can be. The big question is, at your best, who are you?

A group of kids were sitting together at the movie theater when one decided to go to the concession stand. Upon reentering the theater, he couldn't find his group. He walked up and down the aisles, growing more confused with each step. Finally he stood in front of the theater and shouted, "Does anybody recognize me?"

Have you asked kindred questions? Does anyone know who I am? Where I belong? Where I'm supposed to go?

If so, it's time to study your S.T.O.R.Y. and find out! These five questions will help you on your way.

1. What are your strengths? God gave you, not a knapsack, but a knack sack. These knacks accomplish results. Maybe you have a knack for managing multitudes of restaurant orders or envisioning solutions to personnel issues. Synonymous verbs mark your biography: "repairing," "creating," "overseeing." Perhaps you decipher things—Sanskrit or football defenses. Maybe you organize things—data or butterflies. I found my youngest daughter reorganizing her closet, again. *Is this my child?* I wondered. She straightens her closet more often in one month than her father has straightened his in his life! Will she someday do the same in a classroom, medical clinic, or library?

Strengths—you employ them often with seemingly little effort. An interior decorator told me this about her work: "It's not that hard. I walk into a room and begin to see what it needs."

"Not all of us see it," I told her. I can't even decorate my bed. But she can redecorate a garbage dump. Bingo! Knowing her strength led her to her sweet spot. And people pay her to live there! "God has given each of us the ability to do *certain things* well" (Rom. 12:6 NLT).

What certain things come to you so easily that you genuinely wonder why others can't do them? Doesn't everyone know the periodic table of elements? Nooooo, they don't. But the fact that you do says much about your strength (not to mention your IQ!). It also says something about your topic.

2. What is your topic? Once you know your verbs, look for your nouns. What objects do you enjoy working with? Animals? Statistics? People? Your topic can be as abstract as an idea or as concrete as fruit. Arthur Miller Jr. has a friend fascinated by fruit. "Henry," he writes, "not only knows his products, he's downright passionate about them." Miller continues:

> He starts his day in the middle of the night at the wholesale market, buying only high-priced, very good quality produce. He will not buy the ordinary. It is why people come from long distances, and sometimes in chauffeured cars, to tap Henry's passion. His wife says he is a "maniac" about his work. I'll visit Henry to buy a couple of melons, and lightly squeezing a couple of dandies ask, "Are these ripe?" "Not yet!" Henry declares. "Gotta wait until tomorrow." Then he adds, mischievously, "About three o'clock!"
>
> I think he's only half kidding. I think . . . he really does know almost the exact instant when a piece of fruit becomes perfectly ripe! . . .
>
> Imagine if everyone could find the same intensity as . . . Henry Balsamo.[4]

God implants such passion. Listen to the way he described the builder Bezalel. "I have filled him with the Spirit of God, giving him great wisdom, intelligence, and skill in all kinds of crafts. He is able to create beautiful objects from gold, silver, and bronze. He is skilled in cutting and setting gemstones and in carving wood. Yes, he is a master at every craft!" (Exod. 31:3–5 NLT).

That's God speaking! Can you hear the pleasure in his voice? He sounds like a grandpa flipping photos out of his wallet. "I have filled him . . . He is able . . . He is skilled . . . Yes, he is a master." When you do the most what you do the best, you pop the pride buttons on the vest of God.

What fascination did he give you? What makes your pulse race and your eyebrow arch?

3. What are your optimal conditions? What factors trigger your motivation? Some people love to respond to a need. Others are motivated by problems. A competent bookkeeper likely thrives under predictable routine. The firefighter relishes a day packed with different surprises.

> God never called you to be anyone other than you.

So does Dennis McDonald. For a time he served as the business director of our church. He did a fine job. As an elder, however, he often visited the sick. I noticed a distinct difference in enthusiasm when Dennis described his hospital work and his office work. In the office, Dennis soldiered on. He did a fine job managing the routine, but send him to the bedside of the sick, and hear his tone elevate. His optimal setting is crisis, so it made sense to move him from administrator to full-time hospital pastor. A 9-1-1 situation starts his engine.

What starts yours? Building or maintaining? Clearly defined structure or open-ended possibilities? Assembly-line assignments or boundaryless opportunities?

What are your optimal conditions? And . . .

4. What about relationships? Think back over your moments of satisfaction and success. On those days, how were you relating to people?

Some seek out a team, a club, a society. When it comes to yard work, they want the whole family to be outside. Some people are stimulated by groups.

Others function better alone. They pass on the community softball teams or bowling leagues. They prefer to hike or fly-fish or play golf. It's not that they don't like people but more that they don't need people to achieve their assignment.

> You play no small part, because there is no small part to be played.

Still others enjoy a group, but they have to lead the group. In fact, they can't *not* lead the group. They may come across as pushy or domineering, but they don't mean to. They just see what others will see but don't see yet.

Know your ideal relationship pattern. If you like to energize others but your job plops you in front of a computer screen, your days will pass with ice-floe speed. Diagnose your relationship style, and, one final element, determine your payday. What makes you say . . .

5. Yes! In the movie *Chariots of Fire*, Eric Liddell defended his devotion to running by telling his sister, "God made me fast, and when I run, I feel his pleasure." When do you feel God's pleasure? When do you look up into the heavens and say, "I was made to do this"? When do your Strengths, Topic, Optimal conditions, and Relationship pattern converge in such a fashion that you say, "Yes!"? When they do, you are living out your S.T.O.R.Y.

Incarnate yours. Accept God's permission to be whom he made you to be. A frog can flap its little legs and never fly. Some of you have been flapping a long time—too long. Your heroes are birds; your mentors are birds. You think you should fly and feel guilty that you can't. Enough of this bird-brained thinking. Be a frog! It's okay to jump. You have some studdish thighs beneath you, so get hopping.

Do you know who you are? Take a few moments to get acquainted with the S.T.O.R.Y. assessment tool at the back of the book, beginning on page 143. People Management International Inc. developed this process to explore a person's unique giftedness and has successfully used it to guide tens of thousands of people into the right careers. The time you spend quarrying your God-granted skills is well used.

Rick Burgess and Bill "Bubba" Bussey host the wildly popular *Rick and Bubba Show*, a drive-time radio broadcast that originates in Birmingham, Alabama. Animators once made a cartoon out of the two characters and invited Rick and Bubba to provide the voices. Rick was the voice of Rick, and Bubba, the voice of Bubba. Bubba, however, couldn't seem to please his producer. He suggested that Bubba change inflections, volume, and other details. Bubba grew understandably impatient. After all, he was voicing himself. He turned to the producer and objected, "If I am me, how can I mess me up?"[5]

Great point. When it comes to being you, you were made for the part. So speak your lines with confidence.

5

Don't Consult Your Greed

Be content with who you are, and don't put on airs.
God's strong hand is on you; he'll promote you
at the right time.

1 Peter 5:6 MSG

A businessman bought popcorn from an old street vendor each day after lunch. He once arrived to find the peddler closing up his stand at noon. "Is something wrong?" he asked.

A smile wrinkled the seller's leathery face. "By no means. All is well."

"Then why are you closing your popcorn stand?"

"So I can go to my house, sit on my porch, and sip tea with my wife."

The man of commerce objected. "But the day is still young. You can still sell."

"No need to," the stand owner replied. "I've made enough money for today."

"Enough? Absurd. You should keep working."

The spry old man stopped and stared at his well-dressed visitor. "And why should I keep working?"

"To sell more popcorn."

"And why sell more popcorn?"

"Because the more popcorn you sell, the more money you make. The more money you make, the richer you are. The richer you are, the more popcorn stands you can buy. The more popcorn stands you buy, the more peddlers sell your product, and the richer you become. And when you have enough, you can stop working, sell your popcorn stands, stay home, and sit on the porch with your wife and drink tea."

The popcorn man smiled. "I can do that today. I guess I have enough."

I'm rich enough—a phrase on the verge of extinction. We love to super-size our french fries, television screens, and closets—and I've wondered what my dad would say about my penchant for $3.45 lattes.

Who could disagree with Linda Kulman, who wrote:

> We are a nation that believes in having it all. In 1950, American families owned one car and saved for a second. In 2000, nearly 1 in 5 families owned three cars or more. . . . Americans shell out more for garbage bags than 90 of the world's 210 countries spend for everything. Indeed, America has double the number of shopping malls as it does high schools.[1]

In 1900 the average person living in the United States wanted seventy-two different things and considered eighteen of them essential. Today the average person wants five hundred things and considers one hundred of them essential.[2]

Our obsession with stuff carries a hefty price tag. The average American family devotes a full one-fourth of its spendable income to outstanding debts.[3] We spend 110 percent of our disposable income trying to manage debt.[4] And who can keep up? We no longer measure ourselves against the Joneses next door but against the star on the screen or the stud on the maga-zine cover. Hollywood's diamonds make yours look like a gumball-machine toy. Who can satisfy Madison Avenue? No one can. For that reason Jesus warns, "Be on your guard against every form of greed" (Luke 12:15 NASB).

Greed comes in many forms. Greed for approval. Greed for applause. Greed for status. Greed for the best office, the fastest car, the prettiest date. Greed has many faces, but speaks one language: the language of more. Epicurus noted, "Nothing is enough for the man to whom enough is too little."⁵ And what was that observation of John D. Rockefeller's?

He was asked, "How much money does it take to satisfy a man?" He answered, "Just a little more."⁶ Wise was the one who wrote, "Whoever loves money never has money enough; whoever loves wealth is never satisfied with his income" (Eccles. 5:10 NIV).

> Success is not defined by position or pay scale but by this: doing the most what you do the best.

Greed has a growling stomach. Feed it, and you risk more than budget-busting debt. You risk losing purpose. Greed can seduce you out of your sweet spot.

You've seen it happen. The popcorn peddler has one stand and one job and manages both with skill. But though his daily sales meet his needs, they don't meet his tastes. To make more money, he buys more stands; to supervise the stands, he abandons his own.

The street vendor no longer sells; he manages. Which is fine, if he was made to manage. But suppose he was made to sell. Suppose he swaps the open street and river of people for four walls and a desk. Will he give up more than he gains?

God's answer lies in Scripture's first parable. Long before readers pondered the stories of the prodigal son and the good Samaritan, they reflected on the parable of the trees.

Jotham tells the story. He is a son of Gideon and the sole survivor of a seventy-man massacre. Abimelech authorized the slaughter. He sought to kill any person who might keep him from the throne. Jotham comes out of hiding just long enough to address the citizens of Israel and tell them this story:

> Once upon a time the trees decided to elect a king. First they said to the olive tree, "Be our king!" But it refused, saying, "Should I quit producing the olive oil that blesses both God and people, just to wave back and forth over the trees?"
>
> Then they said to the fig tree, "You be our king!" But the fig tree also refused, saying, "Should I quit producing my sweet fruit just to wave back and forth over the trees?"
>
> Then they said to the grapevine, "You be our king!" But the grapevine replied, "Should I quit producing the wine that cheers both God and people, just to wave back and forth over the trees?"
>
> Then all the trees finally turned to the thornbush and said, "Come, you be our king!" And the thornbush replied, "If you truly want to make me your king, come and take shelter in my shade. If not, let fire come out from me and devour the cedars of Lebanon." (Judg. 9:8–15 NLT)

Via the parable, Jotham warns the Israelites against thorny Abimelech. Via the parable, God warns us against greed-driven promotions.

The trees entice the olive tree, fig tree, and grapevine with a throne-room invitation: "Reign over us!" One by one they refuse the offer. The olive tree wants to keep giving oil. The fig tree wants to keep giving figs, and the vine wants to keep bearing grapes. All refuse to pay the price of promotion.

These plants take pride in their posts. Why abandon fruitfulness? In the end, only the thornbush takes the offer.

Be careful, the story instructs. *In a desire to be great, one might cease being any good.*

Not every teacher is equipped to be a principal. Not every carpenter has the skill to head a crew. Not every musician should conduct an orchestra.

Promotions might promote a person right out of his or her sweet spot. For the love of more, we might lose our purpose.

If trees offer you royalty, you don't have to take it. And just because a king gives you armor, you don't have to wear it. David didn't. When he volunteered to go mano a mano with Goliath, King Saul tried to clothe the shepherd boy with soldier's armor. After all, Goliath stood over nine feet tall. He wore a bronze helmet and a 125-pound coat of mail. He bore bronze leggings and carried a javelin and a spear with a 15-pound head (1 Sam. 17:4–7 NLT). And David? David had a slingshot. This is a VW Bug playing blink with an eighteen-wheeler, a salmon daring the grizzly to bring it on. When Saul saw David, pimpled, and Goliath, rippled, he did what any Iron Age king would do. "Saul gave David his own armor—a bronze helmet and a coat of mail" (1 Sam. 17:38 NLT).

> Greed makes a poor job counselor.

But David refused it. Look at this wise young man. "David put it on, strapped the sword over it, and took a step or two to see what it was like, for he had never worn such things before. 'I can't go in these,' he protested. 'I'm not used to them.' So he took them off again" (v. 39 NLT).

David rejected the armor, selected the stones, lobotomized the giant, and taught us a powerful lesson: what fits others might not fit you. Indeed, what fits *the king* might not fit you. Just because someone hands you armor, you don't have to wear it. Just because someone gives you advice, a job, or a promotion, you don't have to accept it. Let your uniqueness define your path of life. "You, Lord, give perfect peace to those who keep their purpose firm and put their trust in you" (Isa. 26:3 TEV).

Examine your gifts; know your strengths. "Have a sane estimate of your capabilities" (Rom. 12:3 Phillips). When someone tries to bump you out of your sweet spot, here is your rebuttal: "This is my S.T.O.R.Y., and I'm sticking to it."

Don't heed greed.

Greed makes a poor job counselor. She tells fig trees to bear no figs, olive trees to bear no oil, vines to bear no grapes. Don't consult her. "Don't be obsessed with getting more material things. Be relaxed with what you have" (Heb. 13:5 MSG). Is not the right job with little better than the wrong job with much? "It is better to have little with fear for the LORD than to have great treasure with turmoil" (Prov. 15:16 NLT). As the Japanese proverb says, "Even if you sleep in a thousand-mat room, you can only sleep on one mat."[7]

> In a desire to be great, one might cease being any good.

Don't let the itch for things or the ear for applause derail you from your God-intended design.

In his book *Money: A User's Manual,* Bob Russell describes a farmer who once grew discontent with his farm. He griped about the lake on his property always needing to be stocked and managed. The hills humped his roads, forcing him to drive up and down. And those fat cows lumbered through his pasture. All the fencing and feeding—what a headache!

He decided to sell the place and move somewhere nice. He called a real-estate agent and made plans to list the farm. A few days later the agent phoned, wanting approval for the advertisement she intended to place in the local paper. She read the ad to the farmer. It described a lovely farm in an ideal location—quiet and peaceful, contoured with rolling hills, carpeted with soft meadows, nourished by a fresh lake, and blessed with well-bred livestock. The farmer said, "Read that ad to me again."

After hearing it a second time, he said, "I've changed my mind. I'm not going to sell. I've been looking for a place like that all my life."[8]

Paul would have applauded that farmer. He learned the same lesson: "I have learned in whatever state I am, to be content" (Phil. 4:11).

Before you change your job title, examine your perspective toward life.

Success is not defined by position or pay scale but by this: doing the most what you do the best.

Parents, give that counsel to your kids. Tell them to do what they love to do so well that someone pays them to do it.

Spouses, urge your mate to choose satisfaction over salary. Better to be married to a happy person who has a thin wallet than a miserable person with a thick one. Besides, "a pretentious, showy life is an empty life; a plain and simple life is a full life" (Prov. 13:7 MSG).

Pursue the virtue of contentment. "Godliness with contentment is great gain" (1 Tim. 6:6 NIV). When choosing or changing jobs, be careful. Consult your design. Consult your Designer. But never consult your greed.

section two
Use your uniqueness

TO MAKE A BIG DEAL OUT OF GOD

every day of your life

Tucked away in the cedar chest of my memory is the image of a robust and rather rotund children's Bible class teacher in a small West Texas church. She wore black eyeglasses that peaked on the corners like a masquerade mask. Silver streaked through her black hair like a vein on the wall of a mine. She smelled like my mom's makeup and smiled like a kid on Christmas when she saw us coming to her class. Low-heeled shoes contained her thick ankles, but nothing contained her great passion. Hugs as we entered and hugs as we left. She knew all six of us by name and made class so fun we'd rather miss the ice-cream truck than Sunday school.

Here is why I tell you about her. She enjoyed giving us each a can of crayons and a sketch of Jesus torn from a coloring book. We each had our own can, mind you, reassigned from cupboard duty to classroom. What had held peaches or spinach now held a dozen or so Crayolas. "Take the crayons I gave you," she would instruct, "and color Jesus." And so we would.

We didn't illustrate pictures of ourselves; we colored the Son of God. We didn't pirate crayons from other cans; we used what she gave us. This was the fun of it. "Do the best you can with the can you get." No blue for the sky? Make it purple. If Jesus's hair is blond instead of brown, the teacher won't mind. She loaded the can.

She taught us to paint Jesus with our own colors.

God made you to do likewise. He loaded your can. He made you unique. But knowing what he gave you is not enough. You need to understand why

51

he gave it: so you could illustrate Christ. Make a big deal out of him. Beautify his face; adorn his image. The next few chapters have one message: color Christ with the crayons God gave you.

Don't waste years embellishing your own image. No disrespect, but who needs to see your face? Who doesn't need to see God's?

Besides, God promises no applause for self-promoters. But great reward awaits God-promoters: "Good work! You did your job well" (Matt. 25:23 MSG). My teacher gave us something similar. Judging by her praise for our sketches, you'd think Rembrandt and van Gogh attended her class. One by one she waved the just-colored Christs in the air. "Wonderful work, Max. Just wonderful!"

I smiled the size of a cantaloupe slice. You will too.

6

Take Big Risks for God

God doesn't want us to be shy with his gifts,
but bold and loving and sensible.

2 Timothy 1:7 MSG

Two families traveled during the same month of the same summer. Both needed a kid to watch their house. Both called me. I was thirteen, unemployed, and broke, so I took the jobs.

I fed their pets (both had dogs), mowed their grass (both had lawns), picked up their daily mail and newspapers (both had both). The jobs were, with one exception, identical. But that one exception proved crucial.

One job scared me. One thrilled me.

I dreaded my time at the Wilson house but relished my time at the Johnson house. The reason for the difference? I didn't know Mr. Wilson. All I knew was what I saw: a tall fence armed with pointed poles; a growling, square-faced bulldog; and a fin-tailed Cadillac, the kind the mobsters drive in movies.

High fence, mean dog, mobster car? Mess up his lawn and prepare to swim in cement. I loathed the Wilson work.

But I loved the Johnson job. He, too, had a fence and a dog. And he drove a truck. A truck often spotted at my house. He knew our family. I knew his laugh, his wife, his favorite quarterback. And since I knew the man, I enjoyed the work.

How you relate to the master of the house colors everything. Dread him and hate your work. Trust him and love it.

How you feel about the Master of the universe does the same. Do you think God treats you with the sensitivity of an Auschwitz prison guard? This assumption guarantees daily deliveries of dread to your heart. Or do you believe God cherishes you like Stradivarius would his newest violin? He does. Believe it, and extract your strengths with great joy.

Jesus made this point in his dramatic parable of the talents:

> For the kingdom of heaven is like a man traveling to a far country, who called his own servants and delivered his goods to them. And to one he gave five talents, to another two, and to another one, to each according to his own ability; and immediately he went on a journey. (Matt. 25:14–15)

Before "talent" meant skill, it meant money. It represented the largest unit of accounting in the Greek currency—10,000 denarii.[1] According to the parable of the workers, a denarius represented a day's fair wages (Matt. 20:2). Multiply your daily wage by 10,000, and you discover the value of a talent. If you earn $30,000 a year and you annually work 260 days, you make about $115 a day. A talent in your case is valued at 10,000 times $115, or $1,150,000.

Place this in perspective. Suppose a person earns $30,000 a year for forty years. Her lifetime earnings are $1,200,000, only $50,000 more than a talent. One talent, then, equals a lifetime of earnings. This is a lot of money and a key point in this parable. Your God-given design and uniqueness have high market value in heaven. God didn't entrust you with a $2 talent or a $5 skill.

Consider yourself a million-dollar investment—in many cases, a multimillion-dollar enterprise.

God gives gifts, not miserly, but abundantly.

And not randomly, but carefully: "to each according to each one's unique ability" (v. 15).[2]

> ## God gives gifts, not miserly, but abundantly.

Remember, no one else has your talents. No one. God elevates you from common-hood by matching your unique abilities to custom-made assignments.

In the parable the first two servants rewarded their master's trust. "Immediately the one who had received the five talents went and traded with them, and gained five more talents. In the same manner the one who had received the two talents gained two more" (vv. 16–17 NASB).

The five-talent servant jumped to the task. He "went and traded" the money. He bought investment magazines and watched the business channel. A reliable tip led him to examine some property. He heard about a franchise looking for capital. He pondered his options, crunched the numbers, took a gulp, and took the plunge. He invested the money.

The second servant showed equal eagerness. He may have had only two talents, but, by George, he put them to work. Like the first servant, he negotiated, traded, and invested.

Both took risks. Both dared to fail. Who was to say their investments wouldn't NASDAQ into pennies? No one. But they took the chance nonetheless.

And their master commended them. When he returned from his journey, he applauded the five-talent man: "Well done, good and faithful servant; you were faithful over a few things, I will make you ruler over many things" (v. 21).

With these words Jesus permits us a glimpse into the end of history, the unannounced day in which the "earth and all its works [will be] exposed to the scrutiny of Judgment" (2 Pet. 3:10 MSG).

"Well done, " Jesus will say to some. Do you not long to be numbered among them? To have your Maker look into your eyes, with all humanity watching and listening, and tell you, "You did a good job"? Maybe your dad never praised you or your teachers always criticized you, but God will applaud you.

And to have him call you "good." When he does, it counts! Only he can make bad sinners good. And only he makes the frail, faithful. "Well done, good and faithful." Not "good and flashy" or "good and famous." Not even "good and fruitful"—just faithful.

Having addressed the five-talent servant, the master turned to the two-talent worker. The master had heaped praise on the $5 million manager. What would he say to the $2 million man? Exactly the same words! "Well done, good and faithful servant; you have been faithful over a few things, I will make you ruler over many things. Enter into the joy of your lord" (Matt. 25:23).

Use your uniqueness to take great risks for God!

He altered no phrase and omitted no honor. The two-talent servant who faithfully fills soda cups for the homeless receives the same applause as the five-talent evangelist who fills stadiums with people. Different fruit, equal praise.

The point? Use your uniqueness to take great risks for God!

If you're great with kids, volunteer at the orphanage.

If you have a head for business, start a soup kitchen.

If God bent you toward medicine, dedicate a day or a decade to AIDS patients.

The only mistake is not to risk making one.

Such was the error of the one-talent servant. Did the master notice him? Indeed, he did. And from the third servant we learn a sobering lesson. "Then he who had received the one talent came and said, 'Lord, I knew you to be a hard man, reaping where you have not sown, and gathering where you have not scattered seed. And I was afraid, and went and hid your talent in the ground'" (vv. 24–25).

Contrast the reaction of the third servant with that of the first two.

The faithful servants "went and traded" (v. 16). The fearful one "went and dug" (v. 18).

The first two invested. The last one buried.

The first two went out on a limb. The third hugged the trunk.

He made the most tragic and common mistake of giftedness. He failed to benefit the master with his talent. All people have talents. This parable, indeed Scripture, assures as much. But how many people invest their gifts to profit the Master?

Many discover their "what." They may luck into "where" to use their "what." But "why"? Why did God pack your bag as he did?

Accountant, how do you explain your number sense?

Investor, you read the stock market like Bobby Fischer reads the chessboard. Ever wondered why you have such a skill?

Linguist, foreign languages paralyze most tongues, but they liberate yours. Why?

And, homemaker, you make your household purr like a Rolls-Royce. For what purpose?

So people will love you? Pay you? Admire you? Hire you? If your answer involves only you, you've missed the big reason, and you're making the big mistake.

Sin, at its ugly essence, confiscates heaven's gifts for selfish gain. C. S. Lewis wrote:

Sin is the distortion of an energy breathed into us—an energy which, if not thus distorted, would have blossomed into one of those holy acts whereof "God did it" and "I did it" are both true descriptions. We poison the wine as He decants it into us; murder a melody He would play with us as the instrument. We caricature the self-portrait He would paint. Hence all sin, whatever else it is, is sacrilege.[3]

While serving in Brazil, I oversaw our small church's benevolence ministry. Needy people walk the streets of Rio de Janeiro. Often they sought our help. We resisted giving them cash but occasionally had no other option. More than once I spotted a person we'd helped earlier in the day staggering from the influence of alcohol. I'd growl at the sight. "I gave him that money to buy food. How dare he use it to get drunk."

Was I wrong to be ticked? No. He misused the gift.

Is the Master wrong to be angry when we do the same? No. And according to this parable, God will be.

Some invest their talents and give God credit. Others misuse their talents and give God grief. Some honor him with fruit. Others insult him with excuses. The one-talent servant did. "I knew you to be a hard man," he said.

The master wouldn't stand for it. Brace yourself for the force of his response. "You wicked and lazy servant, you knew that I reap where I have not sown, and gather where I have not scattered seed. So you ought to have deposited my money with the bankers, and at my coming I would have received back my own with interest" (vv. 26–27).

Whoa. What just happened? Why the blowtorch? Find the answer in the missing phrase. The master repeated the assessment of the servant, word for word, with one exclusion. Did you note it? "I knew you to be a hard man" (v. 24). The master didn't repeat the description he wouldn't accept.

The servant levied a cruel judgment by calling the master a hard man. The servant used the exact word for "hard" that Christ used to describe stiff-necked and stubborn Pharisees (see Matt. 19:8; Acts 7:51). The writer of Hebrews employed the term to beg readers not to harden their hearts (3:8). The one-talent servant called his master stiff-necked, stubborn, and hard.

The only mistake is not to risk making one.

His sin was not mismanagement, but misunderstanding. Was his master hard? He gave multimillion-dollar gifts to undeserving servants; he honored the two-talent worker as much as the five; he stood face to face with both at homecoming and announced before the audiences of heaven and hell, "Well done, good and faithful servant."

Was this a hard master? Infinitely good, graciously abundant, yes. But hard? No.

The one-talent servant never knew his master. He should have. He lived under his roof and shared his address. He knew his face, his name, but he never knew his master's heart. And, as a result, he broke it.

He *could* have known his master. The other servants did. He could have at least asked them. But he didn't. In the end the master instructed: "Get rid of this 'play-it-safe' who won't go out on a limb. Throw him out into utter darkness" (Matt. 25:29–30 MSG).

Jesus refuses to soften the punch line. False servants populate the Master's house. They enjoy his universe, benefit from his earth; they know his name, his habits; they even frequent his presence. But they never know his passion, and as a result they misuse their talents.

Who is this unprofitable servant? If you never use your gifts for God, you are. If you think God is a hard God, you are. And you will live a life of interred talents.

You'll stick your million-dollar skill in a coffee can, hide the can in a drawer, and earn nothing for God. You may use your uniqueness to build a reputation, a retirement, an investment account, or an empire, but you won't build God's kingdom. You may know your S.T.O.R.Y., but you won't share his. As I did with Mr. Wilson, you may cut his grass and feed his dog, but you'll do so with dread. Your heart will grow cold. For fear of doing the wrong thing for God, you'll do nothing for God. For fear of making the wrong kingdom decision, you'll make no kingdom decision. For fear of messing up, you'll miss out. You will give what this servant gave and will hear what this servant heard: "You wicked and lazy servant" (v. 26).

But you don't have to. It's not too late to seek your Father's heart. Your God is a good God.

> GOD is sheer mercy and grace;
>> not easily angered, he's rich in love.
> He doesn't endlessly nag and scold,
>> nor hold grudges forever.
> He doesn't treat us as our sins deserve,
>> nor pay us back in full for our wrongs.
> As high as heaven is over the earth,
>> so strong is his love to those who fear him.
> And as far as sunrise is from sunset,
>> he has separated us from our sins.
> As parents feel for their children,
>> GOD feels for those who fear him.
>
> (Ps. 103:8–13 MSG)

Does this sound like a hardhearted, stiff-necked, stubborn God? By no means. He lavished you with strengths in this life and a promise of the next. Go out on a limb; he won't let you fall. Take a big risk; he won't let you fail. He invites you to dream of the day you feel his hand on your shoulder and his eyes on your face. "Well done," he will say, "good and faithful servant."

Are you certain you will hear these words? If you are, then grab your crayon can and color Christ! If not, take extra time with the next chapter. I wrote it with you in mind. May God use it to guide you to the sweetest spot in the universe, where your best gifts serve the highest purpose: making a big deal out of God.

7

Come to the Sweetest Spot in the Universe

An innocent person died for those who are guilty.
Christ did this to bring you to God.

1 Peter 3:18 CEV

The eighty-seven-year-old man moped through life, living in a sleepy village outside Rome, Italy, with his books and seven cats. His wife had been dead for twelve years, and his only daughter worked in Afghanistan. He lived a dull rhythm, seldom venturing out, rarely speaking to others.

Life was colorless, drab, and lonely. And on the day he decided to do something about it, Giorgio Angelozzi put himself up for adoption. That's right—the octogenarian placed a classified ad in Italy's largest daily newspaper: "Seeks family in need of a grandfather. Would bring 500 euros a month to a family willing to adopt him."

The ad changed his life.

The paper ran a front-page article about him. Inquiries poured in from as far away as Colombia, New Zealand, and New Jersey. Angelozzi became a celebrity overnight. He went from having nothing but time to having scarcely enough time to handle interviews and requests.

A pop star responded. A millionaire offered servants and a seaside villa. But one letter stood out, Angelozzi explained, because every member of the family—father, mother, sister, brother—had signed it.

He settled into their ground-floor apartment, taking walks in the garden, helping with dishes and homework. "I couldn't have chosen better," he says. "Maybe it was luck, or maybe it was God looking after me, I don't know. . . . I knew right away I had found my new home."[1]

The latter option makes the best sense. Heaven never exports monotony. Christ once announced: "I came so they can have real and eternal life, more and better life than they ever dreamed of" (John 10:10 MSG). Nor does God author loneliness. Among our Maker's first recorded words were these: "It is not good for the man to be alone" (Gen. 2:18 NIV).

He gets no argument from us. We may relish moments of solitude—but a lifetime of it? No way. Many of us, however, are too fluent in the language of loneliness.

No one knows me, we think. *People know my name, but not my heart. They know my face, but not my feelings. I have a Social Security number, but not a soul mate. No one really knows me. And . . .*

No one's near me. We hunger for physical contact. Realizing this, two enterprising New Yorkers sell group hugs. You can buy embraces. You can attend a hugfest complete with codes of conduct.[2] Ever since Eve emerged from the bone of Adam, we've been reaching out to touch one another. We need to make a connection. And we need to make a difference.

The anthem of the lonely heart has a third verse: *No one needs me.* The kids used to need me . . . The business once needed me . . . My spouse never needs me . . . Lonely people fight feelings of insignificance.

What do you do with such thoughts? *No one knows me. No one's near me. No one needs me.* How do you cope with such cries for significance?

Some stay busy; others stay drunk. Some buy pets; others buy lovers. Some seek therapy. And a few seek God.

He invites us all to. God's treatment for insignificance won't lead you to a bar or dating service, a spouse or social club. God's ultimate cure for the common life takes you to a manger. The babe of Bethlehem. Immanuel. Remember the promise of the angel? "'Behold, the virgin shall be with child, and bear a Son, and they shall call His name Immanuel,' which is translated, 'God with us'" (Matt. 1:23).

Immanuel. The name appears in the same Hebrew form as it did two thousand years ago. "Immanu" means "with us." "El" refers to Elohim, or God. Not an "above us God" or a "somewhere in the neighborhood God." He came as the "with us God." God with us.

Jesus loved us too much to leave us alone.

Not "God with the rich" or "God with the religious." But God with *us*. All of us. Russians, Germans, Buddhists, Mormons, truckdrivers and taxi drivers, librarians. God with *us*.

God *with* us. Don't we love the word "with"? "Will you go *with* me?" we ask. "To the store, to the hospital, through my life?" God says he will. "I am *with* you always," Jesus said before he ascended to heaven, "to the very end of the age" (Matt. 28:20 NIV). Search for restrictions on the promise; you'll find none. You won't find "I'll be with you if you behave . . . when you believe. I'll be with you on Sundays in worship . . . at mass." No, none of that. There's no withholding tax on God's "with" promise. He is *with* us.

God is with us.

Prophets weren't enough. Apostles wouldn't do. Angels won't suffice. God sent more than miracles and messages. He sent himself; he sent his Son. "The Word became flesh and dwelt among us" (John 1:14).

My niece's husband took a job in another city. During the move he commuted back and forth on weekends for a month. He saw less of his children than any of them would prefer. One evening he called to tell his three-year-old good night. But his son refused to take the phone. "I don't want his voice," he objected. "I want him."

For thousands of years, God gave us his voice. Prior to Bethlehem, he gave his messengers, his teachers, his words. But in the manger, God gave us himself.

Many people have trouble with such a teaching. Islam sees God as one who sends others. He sends angels, prophets, books, but God is too holy to come to us himself. For God to touch the earth would be called a "shirk."[3] People who claim that God has touched the earth shirk God's holiness; they make him gross. They blaspheme him.

> Get the word out. God is with us; we are not alone.

Christianity, by contrast, celebrates God's surprising descent. His nature does not trap him in heaven, but leads him to earth. In God's great gospel, he not only sends, he becomes; he not only looks down, he lives among; he not only talks to us, he lives with us as one of us.

He swims in Mary's womb.

Wiggles in the itchy manger straw.

Totters as he learns to walk.

Bounces on the back of a donkey.

God with us.

He knows hurt. His siblings called him crazy.

He knows hunger. He made a meal out of wheat-field grains.

He knows exhaustion. So sleepy, he dozed in a storm-tossed boat.

He knows betrayal. He gave Judas three years of love. Judas, in turn, gave Jesus a betrayer's kiss.

Most of all, he knows sin. Not his own, mind you. But he knows yours.

Every lie you've told.

Person you've hurt.

Dollar you've taken.

Promise you've broken.

Virtue you've abandoned.

Opportunity you've squandered.

Every deed you've committed against God—for all sin is against God—Jesus knows. He knows them better than you do. He knows their price. Because he paid it. "For Christ also suffered once for sins, the just for the unjust, that He might bring us to God" (1 Pet. 3:18).

Little Blake Rogers can help us understand Jesus's heart-stopping act of grace. He offered a remotely similar gift to his friend Maura. Blake and Maura share a kindergarten class. One day she started humming. Her teacher appreciated the music but told Maura to stop. It's not polite to hum in class.

She couldn't. The song in her head demanded to be hummed. After several warnings, the teacher took decisive action. She moved Maura's clothespin from the green spot on the chart to the dreaded blue spot. This meant trouble.

And this meant a troubled Maura. Everyone else's clothespin hung in the green. Maura was blue, all by herself.

Blake tried to help. He patted her on the back, made funny faces, and offered comforting words. But nothing worked. Maura still felt alone. So Blake made the ultimate sacrifice. Making sure his teacher was watching, he began to hum. The teacher warned him to stop. He didn't. She had no choice but to move his clothespin out of the green and into the blue.

Blake smiled, and Maura stopped crying. She had a friend. And we have a picture, a picture of what Christ did for us.

Color us blue. Every single one of us has sinned a blue streak. Our clips hang from the wrong end of the rope. Our sins have separated us from God. But Jesus loved us too much to leave us alone. Like Blake, he voluntarily passed from green to blue, from righteous to unrighteous.

But here the analogy ceases. Blake took Maura's loneliness, but Christ took so much more. He took our place. He passed from green to blue so that we might pass from blue to green. "For Christ also suffered once for sins, the just for the unjust, that He might bring us to God" (1 Pet. 3:18).

Christ takes away your sin, and in doing so, he takes away your commonness. No longer need you say, "No one knows me." God knows you. He engraved your name on his hands and keeps your tears in a bottle (Isa. 49:16; Ps. 56:8 NASB). "LORD, you . . . know all about me," David discovered. "You know when I sit down and when I get up. You know my thoughts before I think them. You know where I go and where I lie down. You know thoroughly everything I do. . . . You are all around me . . . and have put your hand on me" (Ps. 139:1–3, 5 NCV).

God knows you. And he is near you! How far is the shepherd from the sheep (John 10:14)? The branch from the vine (John 15:5)? That's how far God is from you. He is near. See how these four words look taped to your bathroom mirror: "God is for me" (Ps. 56:9).

> It makes no sense to seek your God-given strength until you trust in his.

And his kingdom needs you. The poor need you; the lonely need you; the church needs you . . . the cause of God needs you. You are part of "the overall purpose he is working out in everything and everyone" (Eph. 1:12 MSG). The kingdom needs you to discover and deploy your unique skill. Use it to make much out of God. Get the word out. God is with us; we are not alone.

The lonely heart of Giorgio Angelozzi drove him to look for a home. He found one. Unfortunately, his home won't last forever. But yours will. Just beyond your grave awaits the place God has prepared for you. "I'll come back and get you," he promised, "so you can live where I live" (John 14:3 MSG).

"God has not destined us for wrath, but for obtaining salvation" (1 Thess. 5:9 NASB). You were born to be saved. Have you let Jesus save you? Think carefully. A person can be religious and yet lost. Attending rodeos won't make you a cowboy. Attending church won't make you God's child. You must accept his offer. Can you point to a day on your life calendar as your day of rescue?

It makes no sense to seek your God-given strength until you trust in his. "It's in Christ that we find out who we are and what we are living for" (Eph. 1:11 MSG). Take a few moments and talk to God. Whether you are making a decision or reaffirming an earlier one, talk to your Maker about your eternal life. You might find this prayer helpful: *Immanuel, you are with me. You became a person and took on flesh. You became a Savior and took on my sin. I accept your gift. I receive you as my Lord, Savior, and friend. Because of you, I'll never be alone again.*[4]

During the writing of this chapter, another picture of God's mercy came my way. The bank sent me an overdraft notice on the checking account of one of my daughters. I encourage my college-age girls to monitor their accounts. Even so, they sometimes overspend.

What should I do? Let the bank absorb it? They won't. Send her an angry letter? Admonition might help her later, but it won't satisfy the bank. Phone and tell her to make a deposit? Might as well tell a fish to fly. I know her liquidity. Zero.

Transfer the money from my account to hers? Seemed to be the best option. After all, I had $25.37. I could replenish her account and pay the overdraft fee as well.

Besides, that's my job. Don't get any ideas. If you're overdrawn, don't call me. My daughter can do something you can't do: she can call me Dad. And since she calls me Dad, I did what dads do. I covered my daughter's mistake.

When I told her she was overdrawn, she said she was sorry. Still, she offered no deposit. She was broke. She had one option. "Dad, could you . . ." I interrupted her sentence. "Honey, I already have." I met her need before she knew she had one.

Long before you knew you needed grace, your Father did the same. He made the deposit, an ample deposit. "Christ died for us while we were still sinners" (Rom. 5:8 NCV). Before you knew you needed a Savior, you had one. And when you ask him for mercy, he answers, "I've already given it, dear child. I've already given it."

And there's more! When you place your trust in Christ, he places his Spirit in you. And when the Spirit comes, he brings gifts, housewarming gifts of sorts. "A spiritual gift is given to each of us as a means of helping the entire church" (1 Cor. 12:7 NLT).

> Before you knew you needed a Savior, you had one.

Remember, God prepacked you with strengths. When you become a child of God, the Holy Spirit requisitions your abilities for the expansion of God's kingdom, and they become spiritual gifts. The Holy Spirit may add other gifts according to his plan. But no one is gift deprived.

Lonely? God is with you.

Depleted? He funds the overdrawn.

Weary of an ordinary existence? Your spiritual adventure awaits.

The cure for the common life begins and ends with God.

8

APPLAUD GOD, LOUD AND OFTEN

Those who worship him must do it out of their very being, their spirits, their true selves, in adoration.

John 4:24 MSG

We suffer from poor I-sight. Not *eye*sight, a matter of distorted vision that lenses can correct, but I-sight. Poor I-sight blurs your view, not of the world, but of yourself.

Some see self too highly. Maybe it's the PhD or pedigree. A tattoo can do it; so can a new truck or the Nobel Peace Prize. Whatever the cause, the result is the same. "I have so many gifts. I can do anything."

Brazenly self-assured and utterly self-sufficient, the I-focused have long strutted beyond the city limits of self-confidence and entered the state of cockiness. You wonder who puts the "air" in arrogance and the "vain" in vainglory? Those who say, "I can do anything."

You've said those words. For a short time, at least. A lifetime, perhaps. We all plead guilty to some level of superiority.

And don't we also know the other extreme: "I can't do anything"?

Forget the thin air of pomposity; these folks breathe the thick, swampy air of self-defeat. Roaches have higher self-esteem. Earthworms stand taller. "I'm a bum. I am scum. The world would be better off without me."

Divorce stirs such crud. So do diseases and job dismissals. Where the first group is arrogant, this group is diffident. Blame them for every mishap; they won't object. They'll just agree and say, "I can't do anything."

Two extremes of poor I-sight. Self-loving and self-loathing. We swing from one side to the other. Promotions and demotions bump us back and forth. One day too high on self, the next too hard on self. Neither is correct. Self-elevation and self-deprecation are equally inaccurate. Where is the truth?

Smack-dab in the middle. Dead center between "I can do anything" and "I can't do anything" lies "I can do all things through Christ who strengthens me" (Phil. 4:13).

Neither omnipotent nor impotent, neither God's MVP nor God's mistake. Not self-secure or insecure, but God-secure—a self-worth based in our identity as children of God. The proper view of self is in the middle.

> The chief reason for applauding God? He deserves it.

But how do we get there? How do we park the pendulum in the center? Counseling? Therapy? Self-help? Long walks? Taking Lucado out to dinner? Advisable activities, but they don't compare with God's cure for poor I-sight:

Worship.

Surprised? The word conjures up many thoughts, not all of which are positive. Outdated songs. Cliché-cluttered prayers. Irrelevant sermons. Meager offerings. Odd rituals. Why worship? What does worship have to do with curing the common life?

Honest worship lifts eyes off self and sets them on God. Scripture's best-known worship leader wrote: "Give honor to the LORD, you angels; give honor to the LORD for his glory and strength. Give honor to the

LORD for the glory of his name. Worship the LORD in the splendor of his holiness" (Ps. 29:1–2 NLT).

Worship gives God honor, offers him standing ovations.

Worship can happen every day in every deed. We can make a big deal about God on Sundays with our songs and on Mondays with our strengths. Each time we do our best to thank God for giving his, we worship. "Take your everyday, ordinary life—your sleeping, eating, going-to-work, and walking-around life—and place it before God as an offering" (Rom. 12:1 MSG). Worship places God on center stage and us in proper posture.

Let me show you how this works.

King David and his men have just raised enough money to build the temple. This is the most successful fund drive ever. *Philanthropy* magazine would happily dedicate an issue to these fund-raisers. They are sitting ducks for cockiness. But before their heads can swell, their knees bow. David leads them in a prayer of worship. Read it slowly:

> Praise be to you, O LORD,
>> God of our father Israel,
>> from everlasting to everlasting.
> Yours, O LORD, is the greatness and the power
>> and the glory and the majesty and the splendor,
>> for everything in heaven and earth is yours.
> Yours, O LORD, is the kingdom;
>> you are exalted as head over all.
> Wealth and honor come from you;
>> you are the ruler of all things.
> In your hands are strength and power
>> to exalt and give strength to all.
> Now, our God, we give you thanks,
>> and praise your glorious name.

But who am I, and who are my people, that we should be able to give as generously as this? Everything comes from you, and we have given you only what comes from your hand. (1 Chron. 29:10–14 NIV)

Imagine a bigheaded guy offering this prayer. He begins arrogantly—his chest puffy and thumbs in lapels—but as the worship continues, reality sets in. As he recites phrases like "Yours . . . is the greatness," "Wealth and honor come from you," "Everything comes from you," he dismounts his high horse. Worship humbles the smug.

By the same token, worship lifts the deflated. Read Psalm 27:10–11, 13–14 to see if the weak wouldn't be strengthened by these words:

> Though my father and mother forsake me,
>> the LORD will receive me.
> Teach me your way, O LORD;
>> lead me in a straight path
>> because of my oppressors. . . .
> I am still confident of this:
>> I will see the goodness of the LORD
>> in the land of the living.
> Wait for the LORD;
>> be strong and take heart
>> and wait for the LORD. (NIV)

Can't you see a head lifting? A back straightening? "The LORD will receive me. . . . I will see the goodness of the LORD." Can you see how these words would turn a face toward the Father and away from frailty?

Worship does that. Worship adjusts us, lowering the chin of the haughty, straightening the back of the burdened.

Breaking the bread, partaking of the cup.

Bowing the knees, lifting the hands.

This is worship.

In the solitude of a corporate cubicle or the community of a church.

Opening our mouths, singing to him our praise.

Opening our hearts, offering to him our uniqueness.

Worship properly positions the worshiper. And oh how we need it! We walk through life so bent out of shape. Five-talent folks swaggering: "I bet God's glad to have me." Two-talent folks struggling: "I bet God's sick of putting up with me." So sold on ourselves that we think someone died and made us ruler. Or so down on ourselves that we think everyone died and just left us.

> Each time we do our best to thank God for giving his, we worship.

Treat both conditions with worship. Cure any flareup of commonness by setting your eyes on our uncommon King.

During our summer vacation I took my daughters on a snorkeling trip. I took advantage of the occasion to solicit a sailing lesson. Ever puzzled by the difference in leeward, starboard, and stern, I asked the crew a few questions. After a while the captain offered, "Would you like to sail us home?" I reminded him that no West Texan has ever won the America's Cup. He assured me I would have no trouble and pointed to a rocky outcrop on the shore. "Target that cliff," he instructed. "Set your eyes and the boat on it."

I found the instruction hard to follow. Other sights invited my attention: the rich mahogany of the deck, my giggling daughters beneath the sail, rich foam cresting on the waves. I wanted to look at it all. But look too long and risk losing the course. The boat stayed on target as long as I set my eyes beyond the vessel.

Worship helps us do this in life. It lifts our eyes off the boat with its toys and passengers and sets them "on the realities of heaven, where Christ sits at God's right hand in the place of honor and power" (Col. 3:1 NLT).

We worship God because we need to.

But our need runs a turtle-paced distant second to the thoroughbred reason for worship.

The chief reason for applauding God? He deserves it. If singing did nothing but weary your voice, if giving only emptied your wallet—if worship did nothing for you—it would still be right to do. God warrants our worship.

How else do you respond to a Being of blazing, blistering, unadulterated, unending holiness? No mark. Nor freckle. Not a bad thought, bad day, or bad decision. Ever! What do you do with such holiness if not adore it?

And his power. He churns forces that launch meteors, orbit planets, and ignite stars. Commanding whales to spout salty air, petunias to perfume the night, and songbirds to chirp joy into spring. Above the earth, flotillas of clouds endlessly shape and reshape; within the earth, strata of groaning rocks shift and turn. Who are we to sojourn on a trembling, wonderful orb so shot through with wonder?

And tenderness? God has never taken his eyes off you. Not for a millisecond. He's always near. He lives to hear your heartbeat. He loves to hear your prayers. He'd die for your sin before he'd let you die in your sin, so he did.

> God would die for your sin before he'd let you die in your sin.

What do you do with such a Savior? Don't you sing to him? Don't you celebrate him in baptism, elevate him in Communion? Don't you bow a knee, lower a head, hammer a nail, feed the poor, and lift up your gift in worship? Of course you do.

Worship God. Applaud him loud and often. For your sake, you need it. And for heaven's sake, he deserves it.

9

JOIN GOD'S FAMILY
OF FRIENDS

God's family is the church of the living God,
the pillar and foundation of the truth.

1 Timothy 3:15 GOD'S WORD

Gary Klahr and Steve Barbin act like brothers.

The two Fairfield, Connecticut, residents look alike, finish each other's
sentences, and speak with the same inflections. Gary served as Steve's best
man. Steve supported Gary through his father's death. They've been insepa-
rable for twenty-five years.

On December 30, 1998, their friendship made sense. A caseworker
called Gary with some personal questions. He thought she wanted to know
if he was interested in adoption. He was partially correct. Her call concerned adoption—his own.

The news came as a bolt from the blue. For fifty-one years he had assumed
he was Benjamin and Marjorie Klahr's biological child. Surprise! And that
discovery was just the beginning.

Gary happened to mention that his friend Steve Barbin was adopted
as well. The caseworker showed instant interest and phoned Steve. "Are

you sitting down? You have a brother," she informed him. "Your friend, Gary Klahr."[1]

Not just buddies, but brothers! Not just friends, but family! How do you imagine these two men felt?

God wants you to find out. He offers you a family of friends and friends who are family—his church. "His unchanging plan has always been to adopt us into his own family by bringing us to himself through Jesus Christ. And this gave him great pleasure" (Eph. 1:5 NLT). When you transfer your trust into Christ, he not only pardons you; he places you in his family of friends.

"Family" far and away outpaces any other biblical term to describe the church. "Brothers" or "brothers and sisters" appears a whopping 148 times between the book of Acts and the book of Revelation.[2] Here are just a few occurrences:

Love the brothers and sisters of God's family. (1 Pet. 2:17 NCV)

Brothers and sisters, now we encourage you to love them even more. (1 Thess. 4:10 NCV)

Keep on loving each other as brothers and sisters. (Heb. 13:1 NCV)

Now that you have made your souls pure by obeying the truth, you can have true love for your Christian brothers and sisters. (1 Pet. 1:22 NCV)

God's family is the church of the living God, the pillar and foundation of the truth. (1 Tim. 3:15 GOD'S WORD)

God is building a family. A permanent family. Earthly families enjoy short shelf lives. Even those that sidestep divorce are eventually divided by death. God's family, however, will outlive the universe. "When I think of the wisdom and scope of his plan I fall down on my knees and pray to the

Father of all the great family of God—some of them already in heaven and some down here on earth" (Eph. 3:14–15 TLB).

> When you transfer your trust into Christ, he not only pardons you; he places you in his family of friends.

Jesus even defined his family according to faith not flesh. "A multitude was sitting around Him; and they said to Him, 'Look, Your mother and Your brothers are outside seeking You.' But He answered them, saying, 'Who is My mother, or My brothers? . . . Whoever does the will of God is My brother and My sister and mother'" (Mark 3:32–33, 35).

Common belief identifies members of God's family. And common affection unites them. Paul gives this relationship rule for the church: "Be devoted to one another in brotherly love" (Rom. 12:10 NIV). The apostle plays the wordsmith here, bookending the verse with fraternal-twin terms. He begins with *philostorgos* (*philos* means friendly; *storgos* means family love) and concludes with *philadelphia* (*phileo* means tender affection; *adelphia* means brethren). An awkward but accurate translation of the verse might be "Have a friend/family devotion to each other in a friend/family sort of way." If Paul doesn't get us with the first adjective, he catches us with the second. In both he reminds us: the church is God's family.

You didn't pick me. I didn't pick you. You may not like me. I may not like you. But since God picked and likes us both, we are family.

And we treat each other as friends.

C. S. Lewis said, "Friendship is born at that moment when one person says to another, 'What! You too? I thought I was the only one.'"[3]

If similar experiences create friendships, shouldn't the church overflow with friendships? With whom do you have more in common than fellow believers? Amazed by the same manger, stirred by the same Bible, saved by the same cross, and destined for the same home. Can you not echo the words of the psalmist? "I am a friend to everyone who fears you, to anyone who obeys your orders" (Ps. 119:63 NCV).

The church. More than family, we are friends. More than friends, we are family. God's family of friends.

Colorado aspens provide a living picture of the church. Have you noticed how they grow in groups, often on the otherwise bald sides of mountains? They are sunseekers and root sharers. Unlike firs or pines, which prefer shade, aspens worship warmth. Unlike oaks, whose roots go deep, aspen roots go wide. They intertwine with other roots and share the same nutrients.

> Our gifts make an eternal difference only in concert with the church.

Light lovers. Root sharers. Sounds like a healthy church.

Oddly, some people enjoy the shade of the church while refusing to set down any roots. God, yes. Church, no. They like the benefits, but resist commitment. The music, the message, the clean conscience—they accept church perks. So they date her, visit her. Enjoy an occasional rendezvous. They use the church. But commit to the church? Can't do that. Got to keep options open. Don't want to miss out on any opportunities.

I propose they already are. Miss the church and miss God's sanctioned tool for God promotion. For church is a key place to do what you do best to the glory of God.

Scripture calls the church a poem. "We are His workmanship" (Eph. 2:10). "Workmanship" descends from the Greek word *poeo* or "poetry." We are God's poetry! What Longfellow did with pen and paper, our Maker does with us. We express his creative best.

You aren't God's poetry. I'm not God's poetry. *We* are God's poetry. Poetry demands variety. "God works through different men in different ways, but it is the same God who achieves his purposes through them all" (1 Cor. 12:6 PHILLIPS). God uses all types to type his message. Logical thinkers. Emotional worshipers. Dynamic leaders. Docile followers. The visionaries who lead, the studious who ponder, the generous who pay the bills. Action-packed verbs. Rock-solid nouns. Enigmatic question marks. Alone, we are meaningless symbols on a page. But collectively, we inspire. "All of you *together* are Christ's body, and each one of you is a separate and necessary part of it" (1 Cor. 12:27 NLT).

All the billions of Christ followers over the last two thousand years have this in common: "A spiritual gift is given to each of us" (1 Cor. 12:7 NLT). God's body has no nobodies. No exceptions. No exclusions. Our gifts make an eternal difference only in concert with the church. Apart from the body of Christ, we are like clipped fingernails, shaved whiskers, and cut hair. Who needs them? No one! They make no contribution. The same applies to our gifts. "Each of us finds our meaning and function as a part of his body" (Rom. 12:5 MSG).

And Christ gave gifts to people—he made some to be apostles, some to be prophets, some to go and tell the Good News, and some to have the work of caring for and teaching God's people. Christ gave those gifts to prepare God's holy people for the work of serving, to make the body of Christ stronger. (Eph. 4:11–12 NCV)

He grants gifts so we can "*prepare* God's holy people." Paul reached into a medical dictionary for this term. Doctors used it to describe the setting of a broken bone.[4] Broken people come to churches. Not with broken bones, but broken hearts, homes, dreams, and lives. They limp in on fractured faith, and if the church operates as the church, they find healing. Pastor-teachers touch and teach. Gospel bearers share good news. Prophets speak words of truth. Visionaries dream of greater impact. Some administer. Some pray.

Some lead. Some follow. But all help to heal brokenness: "to make the body of Christ stronger."

My favorite example of this truth involves an elder in our church, Randy Boggs. He loves the congregation so much he smells like the sheep he tends. Between running a business and raising a family, he encourages the sick and calls on the confused. Few men have kinder hearts. And yet, few men have had their hearts put on ice as his was the night his father was murdered and his stepmother was arrested for his death. She was eventually acquitted, but the deed left Randy with no dad, no inheritance, and no answers.

How do you recover from that? Randy will tell you: through the church. Friends prayed for him, wept with him, stood by him. Finally, after months of wrestling with anger and sorrow, he resolved to move on. The decision came in a moment of worship. God sutured Randy's heart with the lyrics of a hymn. Randy calls it a miracle. That makes two of us.

God heals his family through his family. In the church we use our gifts to love each other, honor one another, keep an eye on troublemakers, and carry each other's burdens. Do you need encouragement, prayers, or a hospitable home?[5] God entrusts the church to purvey these treasures. Consider the church God's treatment center for the common life.

Don't miss it. No one is strong all the time. Don't miss the place to find your place and heal your hurts.

Don't miss the place to find your place and heal your hurts.

Discover what Gary Klahr and Steve Barbin did: friends and family in the same faces. By the way, the caseworker eventually identified that these two brothers had eleven other siblings. A workout partner was Gary's brother, and a former girlfriend was his sister. (That's a scary thought.)

Oh, the immensity, beauty, and surprises of family life.

In God's church, may you find them all.

10

TANK YOUR REPUTATION

Jesus . . . made Himself of no reputation . . . He
humbled Himself and became obedient to the
point of death, even the death of the cross.

Philippians 2:5, 7–8

My teenage acquaintances included a handful of Christians, none of whom were cool. One minister's daughter passed on beer parties and gossip. As a result, she spent most lunch hours and Friday nights alone. A tennis player came back from summer break with a Bible bumper sticker on his car and a smile on his face. We called him a Jesus freak.

My voice was among the mockers. It shouldn't have been, but it was. Somewhere inside I knew better, but I didn't go there for advice. My parents took me to church. My minister told me about Christ. But did I make a big deal about God or the church? No. I had something far more important to promote.

My reputation. An athlete, a flirt, a beer drinker, a partyer. I polished and protected my reputation like a '65 Mustang. What mattered most to me was people's opinion of me.

But then I went off to college and heard a professor describe a Christ I'd never seen. A people-loving and death-defeating Christ. A Jesus who made time for the lonely, the losers . . . a Jesus who died for hypocrites like me. So I signed up. As much as I could, I gave him my heart.

Not long after that decision, I traveled home to meet some of the old gang. Only minutes into the trip I grew nervous. My friends didn't know about my faith. I wasn't sure I wanted them to. I remembered the jokes we had told about the preacher's daughter and the Jesus freak. Did I dare risk hearing the same said about me? Didn't I have my status to protect?

One can't, at once, promote two reputations. Promote God's and forget yours. Or promote yours and forget God's. We must choose.

Joseph did. Matthew describes Jesus's earthly father as a craftsman (Matt. 13:55). He lives in Nazareth: a single-camel map dot on the edge of boredom. Joseph never speaks in the New Testament. He *does* much. He sees an angel, marries a pregnant girl, and leads his family to Bethlehem and Egypt. He does much, but says nothing.

> God grants us an uncommon life to the degree we surrender our common one.

A small-town carpenter who never said a Scripture-worthy word. Is Joseph the right choice? Doesn't God have better options? An eloquent priest from Jerusalem or a scholar from the Pharisees? Why Joseph? A major part of the answer lies in his reputation: he gives it up for Jesus. "Then Joseph [Mary's] husband, being a just man, and not wanting to make her a public example, was minded to put her away secretly" (Matt. 1:19).

With the phrase "a just man," Matthew recognizes the status of Joseph. He was a *tsadiq* (tsa-DEEK), a serious student of the Torah.[1] Nazareth viewed Joseph as we might view an elder, deacon, or Bible class teacher. *Tsadiqs* studied God's law. They recited and lived the *Shema*[2] daily. They supported the synagogue, observed holy days, and followed the food restrictions. For a common carpenter to be known as a *tsadiq* was no small thing. Joseph likely took pride in his standing, but Mary's announcement jeopardized it. *I'm pregnant.*

Mary's parents, by this point, have signed a contract and sealed it with a dowry. Mary belongs to Joseph; Joseph belongs to Mary. Legally and matrimonially bound.

Now what? What's a *tsadiq* to do? His fiancée is pregnant, blemished, tainted . . . he is righteous, godly. On one hand, he has the law. On the other, he has his love. The law says, stone her. Love says, forgive her. Joseph is caught in the middle. But Joseph is a kind man. "Not wanting to disgrace her, [he] planned to send her away secretly" (v. 19 NASB).

A quiet divorce. How long would it stay quiet? Likely not long. But for a time, this was the solution.

Then comes the angel. "While he thought about these things, behold, an angel of the Lord appeared to him in a dream, saying, 'Joseph, son of David, do not be afraid to take to you Mary your wife, for that which is conceived in her is of the Holy Spirit'" (v. 20).

Mary's growing belly gives no cause for concern, but reason to rejoice. "She carries the Son of God in her womb," the angel announces. But who would believe it? Who would buy this tale? Envision Joseph being questioned by the city leaders.

"Joseph," they say, "we understand that Mary is with child."

He nods.

"Is the child yours?"

He shakes his head.

"Do you know how she became pregnant?"

Gulp. A bead of sweat forms beneath Joseph's beard. He faces a dilemma. Make up a lie and preserve his place in the community, or tell the truth and kiss his *tsadiq* good-bye. He makes his decision. "Joseph . . . took to him his wife, and did not know her till she had brought forth her firstborn Son. And he called His name JESUS" (Matt. 1:24–25).

Joseph tanked his reputation. He swapped his *tsadiq* diploma for a pregnant fiancée and an illegitimate son and made the big decision of discipleship. He placed God's plan ahead of his own.

Would you be willing to do the same? God grants us an uncommon life to the degree we surrender our common one. "If you try to keep your life for yourself, you will lose it. But if you give up your life for me, you will find true life" (Matt. 16:25 NLT). Would you forfeit your reputation to see Jesus born into your world?

Consider these situations:

You're a photographer for an ad agency. Your boss wants to assign you to your biggest photo shoot ever. The account? An adult magazine. He knows of your faith. Say yes and polish your reputation. Say yes and use your God-given gift to tarnish Christ's reputation. What do you choose?

The college philosophy teacher daily harangues against Christ. He derides spirituality and denigrates the need for forgiveness. One day he dares any Christian in the class to speak up. Would you?

One more. You enjoy the role of a Christmas Christian. You sing the carols, attend the services . . . Come January, you'll jettison your faith and reshelve your Bible. But during December, you soar.

But this December something hits you. The immensity of it all hits you. *Heaven hung her highest hope and King on a cross, for me.* Radical thoughts begin to surface: joining a weekly Bible study, going on a mission trip, volunteering at a soup kitchen. Your family and friends think you are crazy. Your changing world changes theirs. They want the Christmas Christian back.

You can protect your reputation or protect his. You have a choice.

Joseph made his.

Jesus did too. He "made Himself of no reputation, taking the form of a bondservant, and coming in the likeness of men. And being found in appearance as a man, He humbled Himself and became obedient to the point of death, even the death of the cross" (Phil. 2:7–8).

Christ abandoned his reputation. No one in Nazareth saluted him as the Son of God. He did not stand out in his elementary-classroom photograph, demanded no glossy page in his high-school annual. Friends knew him as a woodworker, not a star hanger. His looks turned no heads; his position earned him no credit. In the great stoop we call Christmas, Jesus abandoned heavenly privileges and aproned earthly pains. "He gave up his place with God and made himself nothing" (Phil. 2:7 NCV).

God hunts for those who will do likewise—Josephs through whom he can deliver Christ into the world.

Deflating inflated egos is so important to God that he offers to help.

He helped me. I recently spent an autumn week on a book tour. We saw long lines and crowded stores. One person after another complimented me. For three days I bathed in the river of praise. I began to believe the accolades. *All these people can't be wrong. I must be God's gift to readers.* My chest puffed so much I could hardly see where to autograph the books. Why, had I been born two thousand years earlier, we might read the gospels of Matthew, *Max*, Luke, and John. About the time I wondered if the Bible needed another epistle, God shot an arrow of humility in my direction.

> Deflating inflated egos is so important to God that he offers to help.

We were running late for an evening book signing, late because the afternoon signing had seen such long lines. We expected the same at the next store. Concerned, we phoned ahead. "We are running behind. Tell all the people we'll arrive soon."

"No need to hurry," the store manager assured.

"What about the people?"

"Neither one seems to be in a hurry."

Neither one?

By the time we reached the store, thankfully, the crowd of two people had tripled to six. We had scheduled two hours for the signing; I needed ten minutes.

Self-conscious about sitting alone at the table, I peppered the last person with questions. We talked about her parents, school, Social Security number, favorite birthday party. Against my pleadings, she had to go. So I sat alone at the table. Big stack of Lucado books, no one in line.

I asked the store manager, "Did you advertise?"

"We did. More than usual." She walked off.

The next time she passed I asked, "Had other signings?"

"Yes, usually we have a great response," and kept going.

I signed all the books at my table. I signed all the Lucado books on the shelves. I signed Tom Clancy and John Grisham books. Finally a customer came to the table. "You write books?" he asked, picking up the new one.

"I do. Want me to sign it?"

"No thanks," he answered and left.

God hit his target. Lest I forget, my daily reading the next morning had this passage: "Do not be wise in your own eyes" (Prov. 3:7).

> When you're full of yourself, God can't fill you.

When you're full of yourself, God can't fill you.

But when you empty yourself, God has a useful vessel. Your Bible overflows with examples of those who did.

In his gospel, Matthew mentions his own name only twice. Both times he calls himself a tax collector. In his list of apostles, he assigns himself the eighth spot.

John doesn't even mention his name in his gospel. The twenty appearances of "John" all refer to the Baptist. John the apostle simply calls himself the "other disciple" or the "disciple whom Jesus loved."

Luke wrote two of the most important books in the Bible but never once penned his own name.

Paul, the Bible's most prolific author, referred to himself as "a fool" (2 Cor. 12:11). He also called himself "the least of the apostles" (1 Cor. 15:9). Five years later he claimed to be "less than the least of all the saints" (Eph. 3:8). In one of his final epistles he referred to himself as the "chief" of sinners (1 Tim. 1:15). As he grew older, his ego grew smaller.

King David wrote no psalm celebrating his victory over Goliath. But he wrote a public poem of penitence confessing his sin with Bathsheba (see Ps. 51).

And then there is Joseph. The quiet father of Jesus. Rather than make a name for himself, he made a home for Christ. And because he did, a great reward came his way. "He called His name JESUS" (Matt. 1:25).

Queue up the millions who have spoken the name of Jesus, and look at the person selected to stand at the front of the line. Joseph. Of all the saints, sinners, prodigals, and preachers who have spoken the name, Joseph, a blue-collar, small-town construction worker, said it first. He cradled the wrinkle-faced Prince of Heaven and, with an audience of angels and pigs, whispered, "Jesus . . . You'll be called Jesus."

Seems right, don't you think? Joseph gave up his name. So Jesus let Joseph say his. You think Joseph regretted his choice?

I didn't regret mine. I went to the hometown party. As expected, everyone asked questions like, "What's the latest?" I told them. Not gracefully or eloquently . . . but honestly. "My faith," I remember saying. "I'm taking faith real seriously."

A few rolled their eyes. Others made mental notes to remove my name from their party list. But one or two found their way over and confided, "I've been thinking the same thing."

Turns out I wasn't standing alone after all.

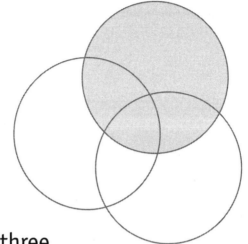

section three

Use your uniqueness
to make a big deal out of God

EVERY DAY
OF YOUR LIFE

Michelangelo was born to sculpt. He once commented that he could taste the tools of a stonecutter in the milk of his wet nurse. He'd sculpted a mature work by the age of twenty-one. By the age of thirty he had produced the still-stunning masterpieces *Pietà* and *David.*

When Michelangelo was in his early thirties, the pope invited him to Rome to complete a special project. Pope Julius II initially asked him to sculpt a papal tomb but then changed his plans and invited him to paint a dozen figures on the ceiling of a Vatican chapel. The sculptor was tempted to refuse. Painting was not his first passion, and a small chapel was not his idea of a great venue. But the pope urged him to accept, so he did. Some historians suspect a setup. Jealous contemporaries convinced the pope to issue the invitation, certain the sculptor would decline and fall into the disfavor of the pontiff.

Michelangelo didn't decline. He began the work. And as he painted, his enthusiasm mounted. Four years, four hundred figures, and nine scenes later, Michelangelo had changed more than the chapel; he'd changed the direction of art. His bold frescoes rerouted the style of European painting. He so immersed himself in the project that he nearly lost his health. "I felt as old and as weary as Jeremiah," he said of his state. "I was only thirty-seven, yet my friends did not recognize the old man I had become."

What happened? What changed him? What turned his work of obligation into an act of inspiration? The answer might lie in a response he gave to a question. An observer wondered why he focused such attention on the details of the corners of the chapel. "No one will ever see them," he suggested.

Michelangelo's reply? "God will."[1]

The artist must have known this passage: "Work with enthusiasm, as though you were working for the Lord rather than for people" (Eph. 6:7 NLT).

God's cure for the common life includes a change in our reporting lines. In this final section I remind you that we have two bosses: one who signs our checks and one who saves our souls. The second has keen interest in our workaday world. What if everyone worked with God in mind? Suppose no one worked to satisfy self or please the bottom line but everyone worked to please God.

Many occupations would instantly cease: drug trafficking, thievery, prostitution, nightclub and casino management. Certain careers, by their nature, cannot please God. These would cease.

Certain behaviors would cease as well. If I'm repairing a car for God, I'm not going to overcharge his children. If I'm painting a wall for God, you think I'm going to use paint thinner?

Imagine if everyone worked for the audience of One. Every nurse, thoughtful. Every officer, careful. Every professor, insightful. Every salesperson, delightful. Every teacher, hopeful. Every lawyer, skillful.

Every corner of every chapel, glistening.

Impossible? Not entirely. All we need is someone to start a worldwide revolution. Might as well be us.

11

Take Your Job and Love It

My heart took delight in all my work.

Ecclesiastes 2:10 NIV

Contrast two workers.

The first one slices the air with his hand, making points, instructing the crowd. He is a teacher and, from the look of things, a compelling one. He stands on a beach, rendering the slanted seashore an amphitheater. As he talks, his audience increases; as the audience grows, his platform shrinks. The instructor steps back and back until the next step will take him into the water. That's when he spots another worker.

A fisherman. Not animated, but frustrated. He spent all night fishing, but caught nothing. All night! Double-digit hours' worth of casting, splashing, and pulling the net. But he caught nothing. Unlike the teacher, the fisherman has nothing to show for his work. He draws no crowds; he doesn't even draw fish. Just nets.

Two workers. One pumped up. One worn-out. The first, fruitful. The second, futile. To which do you relate?

If you empathize with the fisherman, you walk a crowded path. Consider these sobering statistics:

- One-third of Americans say, "I hate my job."
- Two-thirds of your fellow citizens labor in the wrong career.
- Others find employment success, but no satisfaction.[1]
- Most suicides occur on Sunday nights.
- Most heart attacks occur on Monday mornings.[2]

Many people dread their work! Countless commuters begrudge the 83,000 hours their jobs take from their lives. If you're one of them, what can you do?

Change careers? Perhaps. Find one that better fits your design. But until you change, how do you survive? You still have bills to pay and obligations to meet. The problem might be less the occupation and more the outlook toward it. Before you change professions, try this: change your attitude toward your profession.

Jesus's word for frustrated workers can be found in the fifth chapter of Luke's gospel, where we encounter the teacher and the frustrated fisherman. You've likely guessed their names—Jesus and Peter. Random pockets of people populate the Galilean seacoast today. But in the days of Christ, it swarmed, an ant bed of activity. Peter, Andrew, James, and John made their living catching and selling fish. Like other fishermen, they worked the night shift, when cool water brought the game to the surface. And, like other fishermen, they knew the drudgery of a fishless night.

Before you change professions . . . change your attitude toward your profession.

While Jesus preached, they cleaned nets. And as the crowd grew, Christ had an idea.

He noticed two boats tied up. The fishermen had just left them and were out scrubbing their nets. He climbed into the boat that was [Peter's] and asked him to put out a little from the shore. Sitting there, using the boat for a pulpit, he taught the crowd. (vv. 2–3 MSG)

Jesus claimed Peter's boat. He didn't *request* the use of it. Christ didn't fill out an application or ask permission; he simply boarded the boat and began to preach.

He can do that, you know. All boats belong to Christ. Your boat is where you spend your day, make your living, and to a large degree live your life. The taxi you drive, the horse stable you clean, the dental office you manage, the family you feed and transport—this is your boat. Christ shoulder-taps us and reminds:

"You drive my truck."

"You preside in my courtroom."

"You work on my job site."

"You serve my hospital wing."

To us all, Jesus says, "Your work is my work."

Have you seen the painting *The Angelus* by Jean-François Millet? It portrays two peasants praying in their field. A church steeple sits on the horizon, and a light falls from heaven. The rays do not fall on the church, however. They don't fall on the bowed heads of the man and woman. The rays of the sun fall on the wheelbarrow and the pitchfork at the couple's feet.

God's eyes fall on the work of our hands. Our Wednesdays matter to him as much as our Sundays. He blurs the secular and sacred. One stay-at-home mom keeps this sign over her kitchen sink: Divine tasks performed here, daily. An executive hung this plaque in her office: My desk is my altar.

Both are correct. With God, our work matters as much as our worship. Indeed, work can be worship.

Peter, the boat owner, later wrote: "You are a chosen people. You are a kingdom of priests, God's holy nation, his very own possession. This is so you can show others the goodness of God" (1 Pet. 2:9 NLT).

Next time a job application requests your prior employment, write "priest" or "priestess," for you are one. A priest represents God, and you, my friend, represent God. So "let every detail in your lives—words, actions, whatever—be done in the name of the Master, Jesus" (Col. 3:17 MSG). You don't drive to an office; you drive to a sanctuary. You don't attend a school; you attend a temple. You may not wear a clerical collar, but you could. Your boat is God's pulpit.

I have a friend who understands this. By job description she teaches at a public elementary school. By God's description she pastors a class of precious children. Read the e-mail she sent her friends:

I'm asking for your prayers for my students. I know everyone is busy, but if you ever can, I know there is power in specifically addressed prayers. Please pray for . . .

Randy (smartest boy in my class—mom speaks no English—just moved from Washington—blind in his right eye because he poked his eye with a sharp tool when he was three)

Henry (learning disabled—tries with all his little heart—it takes him about a minute to say two words—I think he's used to me now, but it was hard for him to keep up at first!)

Richard (a smile that could almost get him out of any trouble—his mom can't be much older than I am—he's very smart and pretty naughty, just the way I like 'em!)

Anna (learning disability—neither parent can read, write, or drive—they have four children!!! who knows how they keep it together—colors me a picture every single day, writes her spelling sentences about me, I'm the main character in her stories.)

On and on the list goes, including nearly deaf Sara. Disorganized-but-thoughtful Terrell. Model-student Alicia. Bossy-but-creative Kaelyn.

Does this teacher work for a school system or for God? Does she spend her day in work or worship? Does she make money or a difference? Every morning she climbs in the boat Jesus loaned her. The two of them row out into the water and cast nets. My friend imitates Peter. She, however, shows more enthusiasm than he did.

> When [Jesus] finished teaching, he said to Simon [Peter], "Push out into deep water and let your nets out for a catch."
>
> Simon said, "Master, we've been fishing hard all night and haven't caught even a minnow. But if you say so, I'll let out the nets." (Luke 5:4–5 MSG)

Root-canal patients display more excitement. Who can blame Peter? His shoulders ache. His nets are packed away. A midmorning fishing expedition has no appeal. Still, he complies. "I will do as You say and let down the nets" (v. 5 NASB). Hardly hopping up and down. (Nice to know that obedience needn't always wear goose bumps.)

In the light of day, in full sight of the crowd, the fishermen dip their oars and hoist the sail. Somewhere in the midst of the lake, Jesus gives the signal for them to drop their nets, and "it was no sooner said than done—a huge haul of fish, straining the nets past capacity. They waved to their partners in the other boat to come help them. They filled both boats, nearly swamping them with the catch" (vv. 6–7 MSG).

Peter and his cohorts stand knee high in gills. The catch and the message of their lifetimes surround them. What is the message? Some say it's take Jesus to work and get rich! The presence of Christ guarantees more sales, bigger bonuses, longer weekends, and early retirement. With Jesus in your boat, you'll go from Galilean fishing to Caribbean sailing.

But if this passage promises prosperity, Peter missed it. The catch didn't catch his eye. Jesus did. Though surrounded by scales of silver, Peter didn't see dollar signs. He saw Jesus. Not Jesus, the carpenter. Not Jesus, the teacher. Not Jesus, the healer.

Peter saw Jesus, the Lord: mighty enough to control the sea and kind enough to do so from a fisherman's boat. "Simon Peter, when he saw it, fell to his knees before Jesus. 'Master, leave. I'm a sinner and can't handle this holiness. Leave me to myself'" (v. 8 MSG).

> With God, our work matters as much as our worship. Indeed, work can be worship.

What a scene. Christ amid the common grind, standing shoulder to shoulder with cranky workers. Directing fishermen how to fish; showing net casters where to throw. Suppose you were to do what Peter did. Take Christ to work with you. Invite him to superintend your nine-to-five. He showed Peter where to cast nets. Won't he show you where to transfer funds, file the documents, or take the students on a field trip?

Holy Spirit, help me stitch this seam.

Lord of creation, show me why this manifold won't work.

King of kings, please bring clarity to this budget.

Dear Jesus, guide my hands as I trim this hair.

Pray the prayer of Moses: "Let the loveliness of our Lord, our God, rest on us, confirming the work that we do. Oh, yes. Affirm the work that we do!" (Ps. 90:17 MSG).

Hold it there. I saw you roll those eyes. You see no way God could use your work. Your boss has the disposition of a hungry pit bull; hamsters have larger work areas; your kids have better per diems. You feel sentenced to the outpost of Siberia, where hope left on the last train. If so, meet one final witness. He labored eighteen years in a Chinese prison camp.

The Communist regime rewarded his faith in Christ with the sewage assignment. The camp kept its human waste in pools until it fermented into fertilizer. The pits seethed with stink and disease. Guards and prisoners alike avoided the cesspools and all who worked there, including this disciple.

After he'd spent weeks in the pit, the stench pigmented his body. He couldn't scrub it out. Imagine his plight, far from home. And even in the prison, far from people. But somehow this godly man found a garden in his prison. "I was thankful for being sent to the cesspool. This was the only place where I was not under severe surveillance. I could pray and sing openly to our Lord. When I was there, the cesspool became my private garden."

Take Christ to work with you. Invite him to superintend your nine-to-five.

He then quoted the words to the old hymn:

> I come to the garden alone
> While the dew is still on the roses
> And the voice so clear whispers in my ear
> The Son of God discloses.
>
> And He walks with me
> And He talks with me
> And He tells me I am His own
> And the joy we share as we tarry there
> None other has ever known.

"I never knew the meaning of this hymn until I had been in the labor camp," he said.[3]

God can make a garden out of the cesspool you call work, if you take him with you.

Henry Giles, a nineteenth-century preacher, said:

Men and women must work. That is as certain as the sun. But we may work grudgingly or we may work gratefully. We may work as people or machines. There is no work so rude that we may not exalt it; no work so impassive that we may not breathe a soul into it; no work so dull that we may not enliven it if we understand that what we are doing is service for our Lord Jesus Christ.[4]

For Peter and his nets, my friend and her class, the prisoner and his garden, and for you and your work, the promise is the same: everything changes when you give Jesus your boat.

12

PAUSE ON PURPOSE

Come aside by yourselves to
a deserted place and rest a while.

Mark 6:31

Ernie Johnson Jr. knows baseball. His father announced three decades' worth of major-league games, following the Braves from Milwaukee to Atlanta. In the quarter century since Ernie inherited the microphone, he has covered six sports on three continents, voicing blowouts and nail-biters, interviewing losers and buzzer beaters.

But one game stands out above all the rest. Not because of who played, but because of who stopped playing. Ernie was a nine-year-old Little Leaguer, dutifully playing shortstop. An opposing batter hit a ground rule double that bounced over the fence. Two outfielders scampered over the fence to retrieve the ball so the game could continue. (Apparently the league operated on a tight budget.)

Both teams waited for them to return. They waited . . . and waited . . . but no one appeared. Concerned coaches finally jogged into the outfield and scaled the fence. Curious players, including Ernie, followed them. They found the missing duo just a few feet beyond the fence, gloves dropped on the ground, found ball at their feet, blackberries and smiles on their faces.[1]

The two players had stepped away from the game.

How long since you did the same? To stay sweet spot centered you must. The devil is determined to bump you out of your strengths. We need regular recalibrations. Besides, who couldn't use a few blackberries? But who has time to gather them? You have carpools to run; businesses to run; sales efforts to run; machines, organizations, and budgets to run. You gotta run.

Jesus understands. He knew the frenzy of life. People back-to-backed his calendar with demands. But he also knew how to step away from the game.

When the sun was setting, all those who had any that were sick with various diseases brought them to Him; and He laid His hands on every one of them and healed them. And demons also came out of many, crying out and saying, "You are the Christ, the Son of God!" And He, rebuking them, did not allow them to speak, for they knew that He was the Christ.

Now when it was day, He departed and went into a deserted place. And the crowd sought Him and came to Him, and tried to keep Him from leaving them; but He said to them, "I must preach the kingdom of God to the other cities also, because for this purpose I have been sent." And He was preaching in the synagogues of Galilee. (Luke 4:40–44)

These words document Jesus's entry into the public arena. Having withstood the devil's wilderness temptation and his hometown's harsh rejection, Jesus journeyed to Capernaum, where the citizens gave him a ticker-tape reception. Think John Kennedy at the 1960 Democratic National Convention. (Young hope has arrived.)

They were astonished at His teaching. (Luke 4:32)

The story of what he had done spread like wildfire throughout the whole region. (v. 37 NLT)

People throughout the village brought sick family members to Jesus. No matter what their diseases were, the touch of his hand healed every one. (v. 40 NLT)

Could Christ have wanted more? Enthralled masses, just-healed believers, and thousands who would follow his lead. So Jesus . . .

Rallied a movement?

Organized a leadership team?

Mobilized a political-action society?

No. He baffled the public-relations experts by placing the mob in the rearview mirror and ducking into a wildlife preserve, a hidden cove, a vacant building, a *deserted place.*

Verse 42 identifies the reason: "the crowd . . . tried to keep Him from leaving them." People brought Jesus more than sick bodies and seeking souls. They brought him agendas. Itineraries. Unsolicited advice. The herd of humanity wanted to set Jesus's course. "Heed us," they said. "We'll direct your steps."

> The devil is determined to bump you out of your strengths.

They say the same to you. Look over your shoulder, my friend. The crowd is one step back. They don't consult your strengths or know your S.T.O.R.Y. Still, they seem to know more about your life than you do. Where you should work. Whom you should marry. What you should study. They will lead your life if you allow them.

Jesus didn't.

More than once he exercised crowd control. "When Jesus saw the crowd around him, he told his followers to go to the other side of the lake" (Matt. 8:18 NCV).

When the crowd ridiculed his power to raise a girl from the dead, he evicted them from the premises. "After the crowd had been thrown out of the house, Jesus went into the girl's room and took hold of her hand, and she stood up" (Matt. 9:25 NCV).

After a day of teaching, "Jesus left the crowd and went into the house" (Matt. 13:36 NCV).

Though surrounded by possibly twenty thousand fans, he turned away from them: "After Jesus had sent the crowds away" (Matt. 15:39 CEV).

Christ repeatedly escaped the noise of the crowd in order to hear the voice of God. After his forty-day pause in the wilderness, the people of Capernaum "tried to keep Him from leaving them; but He said to them, 'I must preach the kingdom of God to the other cities also, because for this purpose I have been sent'" (Luke 4:42–43).

He resisted the undertow of the people by anchoring to the rock of his purpose: employing his uniqueness (to "preach . . . to the other cities also") to make a big deal out of God ("the kingdom of God") everywhere he could.

And aren't you glad he did? Suppose he had heeded the crowd and set up camp in Capernaum, reasoning, "I thought the whole world was my target and the cross my destiny. But the entire town tells me to stay in Capernaum. Could all these people be wrong?"

Yes, they could! In defiance of the crowd, Jesus turned his back on the Capernaum pastorate and followed the will of God. Doing so meant leaving some sick people unhealed and some confused people untaught. He said no to good things so he could say yes to the right thing: his unique call.

Not an easy choice for anyone. It wasn't for me. May I describe how a purposeful pause pulled me out of a spiritual desert?

I can't blame my drought on the church. Attendance was soaring, enthusiasm mounting. We had outgrown our building and set our eyes on new property. Everyone pulled together to raise money and make plans. After two years of prayer and plans, gauntlets and victories, we made the move.

And it nearly did me in. I remember standing in the new building before our beaming congregation, thinking, *I should be thrilled.* Instead, I was hollow, robotic, and mechanical. A friend noticed. (Thank God for friends who do.) He convinced me to do what this book urges you to do: clarify my sweet spot.

Under the tutelage of executive coach and organizational consultant Rick Wellock, I wrote out my S.T.O.R.Y. "Describe some occasions when you did something you love to do and did it well" was my assignment. I reviewed my life, listing events of intersected satisfaction and success.

> Jesus said no to good things so he could say yes to the right thing.

As an elementary student, reading every biography in the school library.

Delivering an election-winning speech to the high-school freshman class.

Neglecting other homework so I could write and rewrite short stories for a literature course.

Presenting my first Bible lesson. Stunned that the middle-schoolers listened.

Developing a detailed procedure for sermon preparation.

I devoted an entire day to passion review. After the counselor studied my reflections, he asked, "What one word describes your sweet spot?"

"Message," I replied without hesitation. I realized I exist to reflect God through clear teaching and compelling stories.

He then asked the question that undid me. "Does your calendar reflect your passion?"

We reviewed the previous six months of meetings, fund-raising, and facility development. "Seems like you are sitting on a lot of planning committees," he observed.

"I assumed I should since I'm the minister."

"Tell me, what do you discuss in these meetings?"

"Paint color. Parking lot size. City building codes."

"Do you enjoy them?"

"Slightly more than open-heart surgery."

"Does your S.T.O.R.Y. include any successfully supervised construction projects?"

"No."

"Do people ever turn to you for strategic-planning advice?"

"No."

"Then what makes you think you should be giving it now?"

My exhaustion made sudden sense. I was operating out of my weakness, doing the most what I do the worst! With lesson learned, I resigned from every committee and returned to study and writing. In short order, energy resurged, and passion rekindled. Renewal began when I paused on purpose.[2]

What about you? Do you sense a disconnect between your design and daily duties? Are you neglecting your strengths? God may want you to leave your Capernaum, but you're staying. Or he may want you to stay, and you're leaving. How can you know unless you mute the crowd and meet with Jesus in a deserted place?

> Christ repeatedly escaped the noise of the crowd in order to hear the voice of God.

"Deserted" need not mean desolate, just quiet. Simply a place to which you, like Jesus, *depart*. "Now when it was day, He departed" (Luke 4:42). "Depart" presupposes a decision on the part of Jesus. "I need to get away. To think. To ponder. To rechart my course." He determined the time, selected a place. With resolve, he pressed the pause button on his life.

Your escape requires equal determination. Hell hates to see you stop! Richard Foster hit the mark when he wrote: "In contemporary society our Adversary majors in three things: noise, hurry, and crowds. If he can keep us engaged in 'muchness' and 'manyness,' he will rest satisfied. Psychiatrist C. G. Jung once remarked, 'Hurry is not *of* the Devil; it *is* the Devil.'"[3]

The devil implants taximeters in our brains. We hear the relentless tick, tick, tick telling us to hurry, hurry, hurry, time is money . . . resulting in this roaring blur called the human *race.*

But Jesus stands against the tide, countering the crescendo with these words: "Come to Me, all you who labor and are heavy laden, and I will give you rest" (Matt. 11:28). Follow the example of Jesus, who "often withdrew into the wilderness and prayed" (Luke 5:16).

Eugene Peterson sets a healthy example here. This multibook author and three-decade pastor knows the importance of pausing on purpose. He wrote:

Monday is my sabbath. Nothing is scheduled for Mondays. If there are emergencies I respond, but there are surprisingly few. My wife joins me in observing the day. We make a lunch, put it in a daypack, take our binoculars and drive anywhere from fifteen minutes to an hour away, to a trailhead along a river or into the mountains. Before we begin our hike my wife reads a psalm and prays. After that prayer there is no more talking—we enter into a silence that will continue for the next two or three hours, until we stop for lunch.

We walk leisurely, emptying ourselves, opening ourselves to what is there: fern shapes, flower fragrance, birdsong, granite outcropping, oaks and sycamores, rain, snow, sleet, wind. . . . When the sun or our stomachs tell us it is lunch time, we break the silence with a prayer of blessing for the sandwiches and fruit, the river and the forest. We are free to talk now, sharing bird sightings, thoughts, observations, ideas—however much or little we are inclined. We return home in the middle or late afternoon, putter, do odd jobs, read. After supper I usually write family letters. That's it. No Sinai thunder. No Damascus Road illuminations. No Patmos visions. A day set apart for solitude and silence. Not-doing. Being-there. The sanctification of time.[4]

Dr. Peterson's words have inspired me. I now own a walking stick and a wide-brimmed hat. A favorite trail in a nearby nature park knows the feel of my steps. I'm a remedial student in the course of pausing, but my grades are improving. A church member asked me after a recent service, "Did I see you sitting on a park bench?"

"Yes."

"In the middle of the day?"

The old Max would have justified the appearance of laziness. "Studying. Just getting some work done." But I offered no excuse. "That was me. Just resting." He gave a curious look and moved on. I smiled to myself, pleased to have set a saner example. God rested after six days of work, and the world didn't collapse. What makes us think it will if we do? (Or do we fear it won't?)

Follow Jesus into the desert. A thousand and one voices will scream like banana-tree monkeys telling you not to. Ignore them. Heed him. Quit your work. Contemplate his. Accept your Maker's invitation: "Come aside by yourselves to a deserted place and rest a while" (Mark 6:31).

And while you are there, enjoy some blackberries.

13

TRUST
LITTLE DEEDS

Do not despise these small beginnings.

Zechariah 4:10 NLT

World War II had decimated Germany. Citizens clamored for supplies. Russia reduced Berlin's buildings to skeletons and sought to do the same to her people. They blockaded food-bearing trucks, trains, and boats. Without help, the city would starve. The U.S. and British military responded with the 1948 airlift. For eleven months, they airdropped tons of food to the 2.5 million Berliners.

Gail Halvorsen piloted one of the planes for the United States. After landing in Berlin one day, the twenty-seven-year-old talked with thirty or so German children through a barbed-wire fence. Though hungry and needy, they didn't beg or complain.

Impressed, Halvorsen reached into his pocket, produced two sticks of gum, broke them in half, and handed the pieces through the wire. "Those kids looked like they had just received a million bucks," he recounted. "They put that tiny piece of paper to their noses and smelled the aroma. They were on cloud nine. I stood there dumbfounded."

Touched by their plight, Halvorsen promised to return the next day and drop more gum from his plane. With supply flights landing every half hour, the children asked how they'd recognize him. "I'll wiggle my wings," he replied.

Halvorsen returned to Rhein-Main Air Force Base and bought gum and candy rations from his buddies. He tied the sweets to tiny handkerchief parachutes, loaded them on his C-54, and, true to his word, wiggled his wings over Berlin. Kids in the city streets spotted their friend and ran to gather the falling candy.

Operation Little Vittles had begun. Momentum mounted quickly. Within three weeks the air force sanctioned the crusade. During the following months, U.S. planes dropped three tons of candy on the city. The pilot became known as Uncle Wiggly Wings.[1]

Do small deeds make big differences? Halvorsen thinks they do.

Of greater importance, Jesus does. He says:

"The Kingdom of Heaven is like a mustard seed planted in a field. It is the smallest of all seeds, but it becomes the largest of garden plants and grows into a tree where birds can come and find shelter in its branches."

Jesus also used this illustration: "The Kingdom of Heaven is like yeast used by a woman making bread. Even though she used a large amount [three measures] of flour, the yeast permeated every part of the dough." (Matt. 13:31–33 NLT)

Original readers caught quickly the pictures of this parable. They knew mustard seeds and leaven lumps. Both were small: the seed the size of a freckle (it takes 750 to weigh one gram[2]), the leaven no larger than the end of your thumb. Yet a tiny mustard seed can erupt and reach for the clouds, growing to three times the average height of the ancient Jew, boasting bushy branches large enough to house a homeless flock of birds. A pinch of fermented dough can feed forty people three meals a day for several days. What begins minutely ends massively.

Maybe the early church needed this reminder. What clout do a tiny manger and a bloody cross carry in a forest of Jewish tradition and Greek philosophy? How can a backwoods movement headed by a rural carpenter gain traction in a religious world dominated by Epicureans, Stoics, and Gnostics? This is a kid on a skateboard entering the Daytona 500.

Don't we need a reminder today? We, at times, fear the smallness of Jesus's story. Our fear might keep us from seed sowing. Can the Sunday school account of Jesus hold its own in the Ivy League? Do terms like "sin," "salvation," and "redemption" stand a chance in this sophisticated day of humanism and relativism?

> Just do something and see what happens.

Apparently they do. Where are the Romans who crucified Christ? The Epicureans who demeaned and debated Paul? The Gnostics who mocked the early church? And the great temples of Corinth? They dwarfed the infant church. Do worshipers still sacrifice to Zeus?

No, but they still sing to Jesus.

God does uncommon works through common deeds.

A friend of mine saw proof of this truth as he cared for victims of Hurricane Katrina. Being a physician, he gave his time and talent to treat some of the 12,500 New Orleans evacuees who ended up in San Antonio.

One survivor told him a riveting story. As the waters rose around his house, this New Orleanian swam out a window. With two children clinging to his back, the man found safe refuge atop the tallest building in the neighborhood. Other people joined him on the roof. Soon a small circle of people huddled together on what would be their home for three days until they were rescued.

After an hour on the building, the man realized he was on a church. He patted the rooftop and announced to the others, "We are on holy ground." His news jogged the memory of another roof dweller. She looked around at the area, crawled over to the steeple, hugged it, and proclaimed, "My grandfather and grandmother helped build this church!"

Do you think those grandparents ever imagined God would use their work to save their granddaughter? They surely prayed for God to use that building to save souls . . . but they couldn't have imagined he would use it to save their grandchild from a hurricane. They had no idea how God would use the work of their hands.

Nor do you.

What difference do selfless deeds make? Do you wonder if your work makes a difference? I'm envisioning a reader at the crossroads. One recently impacted by God, perhaps through this book. The divine spark within is beginning to flame. Should you douse it or fan it? Dare you dream that you can make a difference?

God's answer would be, "Just do something and see what happens."

That's what he told the citizens of ancient Jerusalem. For sixteen years the temple of God had lain in ruins. They had abandoned the work. The reason? Opposition from enemies, indifference from neighbors. But most of all, the job dwarfed them. To build the first temple, Solomon had needed seventy thousand carriers, eighty thousand stonecutters, thirty-three hundred foremen, and seven years. A gargantuan task! The workers must have thought, *What difference will my work make?* God's answer: "Do not despise these small beginnings, for the LORD rejoices to see the work *begin*" (Zech. 4:10 NLT).

> "The LORD rejoices to see the work begin."

Begin. Just begin! What seems small to you might be huge to someone else. Just ask Bohn Fawkes. During World War II, he piloted a B-17. On one mission he sustained flak from Nazi antiaircraft guns. Even though his gas tanks were hit, the plane did not explode, and Fawkes was able to land the plane.

On the morning following the raid, Fawkes asked his crew chief for the German shell. He wanted to keep a souvenir of his incredible good fortune. The crew chief explained that not just one but eleven shells had been found in the gas tanks, none of which had exploded.

Technicians opened the missiles and found them void of explosive charge. They were clean and harmless and with one exception, empty. The exception contained a carefully rolled piece of paper. On it a message had been scrawled in the Czech language. Translated, the note read: "This is all we can do for you now."[3]

A courageous assembly-line worker was disarming bombs and scribbled the note. He couldn't end the war, but he could save one plane. He couldn't do everything, but he could do something. So he did it.

God does big things with small deeds.

Against a towering giant, a brook pebble seems futile. But God used it to topple Goliath. Compared to the tithes of the wealthy, a widow's coins seem puny. But Jesus used them to inspire us. And in contrast with sophisticated priests and powerful Roman rulers, a cross-suspended carpenter seemed nothing but a waste of life. Few Jewish leaders mourned his death. Only a handful of friends buried his body. The people turned their attention back to the temple. Why not?

Don't discount the smallness of your deeds.

What power does a buried rabbi have? We know the answer. Mustard-seed and leaven-lump power. Power to tear away death rags and push away death rocks. Power to change history. In the hands of God, small seeds grow into sheltering trees. Tiny leaven expands into nourishing loaves.

Small deeds can change the world. Sow the mustard seed. Bury the leaven lump. Make the call. Write the check. Organize the committee. Drop some gum from your airplane. Sixty years from now another soldier might follow your example. Chief Wiggles did.

No, not Uncle Wiggly Wings of Berlin fame, but Chief Wiggles of Iraq. Like Halvorsen, his story begins with a child at a fence. And like the candy bomber, his work began by giving one gift.

He noticed a little girl crying on the other side of a stretch of barbed wire in Baghdad. "She was obviously very poor, in her tattered old dress, totally worn out plastic flip-flops, her hair matted against her head indicating she hadn't had a bath in a long time and her skin blistered from the dirt and weather." The soldier remembered some toys in his office, so he hurried and brought the girl a toothbrush, whistle, and toy monkey. As he gave the gifts, "her eyes lit up with such joy." He posted this experience on his Weblog, and thousands of people responded, asking where they could send gifts. Operation Give was born. And the soldier inherited Halvorsen's nickname—"Chief Wiggles."[4]

Moses had a staff.

David had a sling.

Samson had a jawbone.

Rahab had a string.

Mary had some ointment.

Aaron had a rod.

Dorcas had a needle.

All were used by God.

What do you have?

God inhabits the tiny seed, empowers the tiny deed. He cures the common life by giving no common life, by offering no common gifts. "Do all the good you can, by all the means you can, in all the ways you can, in all the places you can, at all the times you can, to all the people you can, as long as ever you can."[5] Don't discount the smallness of your deeds.

14

DECODE YOUR KID'S CODE

I am your Creator. You were in my care
even before you were born.

Isaiah 44:2 CEV

A gardener gave a seedling to his friend, the orange grower. "Consider this a gift."

An orchestra conductor presented a package to her favorite cellist. "Just because I appreciate your work," she told her.

An artist thanked a plumber for his neighborliness by giving him a present.

And so the orange grower, the cellist, and the plumber unwrapped their gifts.

The orange grower planted the seedling, anticipating oranges. After all, he grew oranges, so this must be an orange-tree-to-be. But the plant spread into bushy, clustered branches. The orange grower couldn't coax a single orange out of his grove. He sprinkled it with orange-tree fertilizer, sprayed it with orange-tree bug spray. He even poured orange juice on the soil. But, alas, no oranges. Tomatoes, yes. But oranges, no. He felt like a failure.

The cellist empathized. She had expected a cello. She was somewhat correct. The package contained an accordion. She treated the accordion like a cello, setting the base on the floor and running her bow across the keys. Noise came forth, but no music. She was less than enthused.

As was the plumber. He expected a gift of wrenches and hammers, but he was given a brush and palette. Puzzled, he set out to repair a leaky pipe with his new tools. But brushes don't open valves, and a palette won't tighten joints. He painted the plumbing and grumbled.

The orange grower raised the tomatoes, but preferred oranges.

The cellist made sounds, but not music.

The plumber painted the pipe, but didn't fix it.

Each assumed the gift would be what they knew rather than what the giver gave.

Each year God gives millions of parents a gift, a brand-new baby. They tend to expect oranges, cellos, and plumbing tools. Heaven tends to distribute tomatoes, accordions, and paint supplies. Moms and dads face a decision. Make our children in our images? Or release our children to follow their God-given identities?

> Like no one else, parents can unlock the door to a child's uncommonness.

Like no one else, parents can unlock the door to a child's uncommonness. As parents, we accelerate or stifle, release or repress our children's giftedness. They will spend much of life benefiting or recovering from our influence. Though not a book on parenting, this book deserves a word for moms and dads. Who has a greater chance of helping our children live in their sweet spots than we do? But will we?

God's Word urges us to. Listen closely to this maternity-ward reminder: "Train up a child in the way he should go, and when he is old he will not depart from it" (Prov. 22:6).

Be careful with this verse. Don't interpret it to mean "If I put my kids on the right path, they'll never leave it. If I fill them full of Scripture and Bible lessons and sermons, they may rebel, but they'll eventually return."

The proverb makes no such promise. Salvation is a work of God. Godly parents can prepare the soil and sow the seed, but God gives the growth (1 Cor. 3:6). Moms and dads soften hearts, but can't control them. Show them the path? Yes. Force them to take it? No.

Then what does this passage teach parents?

To learn to love tomatoes,

    appreciate the sound of an accordion,

        take art supplies to the canvas, not the sink, and

            view each child as a book, not to be written, but to be read.

The phrase "train up" descends from a root word that means to develop a thirst. Hebrew midwives awakened the thirst of a newborn by dipping a finger in a bowl of crushed dates and placing it in the baby's mouth. To "train up," then, means to awaken thirst.

Parents awaken thirst "in the way [the child] should go." The small word "in" means "in keeping with" or "in cooperation with," suggesting that babies come with preprogrammed hard drives. The American Standard Bible margins this verse with the phrase "according to his way."

In Hebrew, "way" suggests "manner" or "mode." Look at the same word in Proverbs 30:18–19 (NASB):

> There are three things which are too wonderful for me,
>
> Four which I do not understand:
>
> The *way* of an eagle in the sky,
>
> The *way* of a serpent on a rock,
>
> The *way* of a ship in the middle of the sea,
>
> And the *way* of a man with a maid.

"Way" refers to a unique capacity or characteristic, whether of an eagle, a serpent, a ship, or a person. If you raise your child "in *the way* he should go," you attune yourself to your child's inherent characteristics and inborn distinctives.

"Way" can also mean "bent." The psalmist uses it to describe the bent or bending bow:

[God] has bent His bow and made it ready. (Ps. 7:12 NASB)

For, behold, the wicked bend the bow,

They make ready their arrow upon the string

To shoot in darkness at the upright in heart. (Ps. 11:2 NASB)

The archer arches the weapon, setting his aim on a target. By the time your child is born, God has done the same. He has already "bent" your child in a certain direction. He hands you a preset bow that you secure until the day of release. Raise your child in the way "he should go." Read your child's God-designed itinerary. Don't see your child as a blank slate awaiting your pen, but as a written book awaiting your study.

The Amplified Bible translates this verse: "Train up a child in the way he should go [and in keeping with his individual gift or bent], and when he is old he will not depart from it."

Charles Swindoll's fine book *You and Your Child* serves as a great resource for parents. He writes:

In every child God places in our arms, there is a *bent,* a set of characteristics already established. The bent is fixed and determined before he is given over to our care. The child is not, in fact, a pliable piece of clay. He has been set; he has been bent. And the parents who want to train this child correctly will discover that bent![1]

God prewired your infant. He scripted your toddler's strengths. He set your teen on a trajectory. God gave you an eighteen-year research project. Ask yourself, your spouse, and your friends: what sets this child apart? Childhood tendencies forecast adult abilities. Read them. Discern them. Affirm them. Cheerlead them.

An example. Eight-year-old R. G. Collingwood sits wedged between his father's bookcase and table, reading, of all things, *Kant's Theory of Ethics*. He later wrote:

> As I began reading it, . . . I was attacked by a strange succession of emotions. . . . I felt that the contents of this book, although I could not understand it, were somehow my business; a matter personal to myself, or rather to some future self of my own. . . . I felt as if a veil had been lifted and my destiny revealed.[2]

His hunch proved true. By the time of his death in 1943, Collingwood had established himself as a distinguished philosopher with works in metaphysics, religion, and aesthetics.

Immanuel Kant entrances few eight-year-olds. But every eight-year-old is entranced with something. And that "something" says something about God's intended future for the child.

Look at Joseph. At the age of seventeen, he interpreted dreams and envisioned himself as a leader (Gen. 37:2–10). As an adult he interpreted the dreams of Pharaoh and led the nation of Egypt (Gen. 40–41).

Young shepherd-boy David displayed two strengths: fighting and music. He killed a lion and a bear (1 Sam. 17:34–37) and played the harp with skill (16:18). What two activities dominated his adult years? Fighting and music. He killed tens of thousands in battle (29:5), and do we not still sing his songs?

Even Jesus displayed an early bent. Where did Joseph and Mary locate their lost twelve-year-old? "Now so it was that after three days they found

Him in the temple, sitting in the midst of the teachers, both listening to them and asking them questions" (Luke 2:46). Joseph the carpenter didn't find his son among carpenters, but among teachers of faith and interpreters of the Torah. Did this early interest play out later in life? By all means. Even his enemies referred to him as "Rabbi" (Matt. 26:49). Jesus, the son of a carpenter, displayed the heart of a rabbi.

In fact, do we detect a mild rebuke in his response to his parents? "And He said to them, 'Why did you seek Me? Did you not know that I must be about My Father's business?'" (Luke 2:49). He may have been saying, "You should have seen my bent. I've been under your roof for twelve years. Don't you know my heart?"

Don't see your child as a blank slate awaiting your pen, but as a written book awaiting your study.

What about your children? Do you know their hearts? What are their S.T.O.R.Y.'s?

Strengths. What abilities come easily for them? At the age of two, master pianist Van Cliburn played a song on the piano as a result of listening to teaching in the adjacent room. His mother noticed this skill and began giving him daily piano lessons. The little kid from Kilgore, Texas, won the First International Tchaikovsky Piano Competition in Moscow. Why? In part because a parent noticed an aptitude and helped a child develop it.[3]

Topics. Writer John Ruskin said, "Tell me what you like and I'll tell you what you are."[4] What do your children like? What projects enrapture them? In which topics are they delightfully lost? Numbers? Colors? Activities?

A photograph of my three-year-old great-nephew, Lawson, appeared in our city's paper. He spotted two equally glorious sights on a San Antonio sidewalk: a mariachi band and a display of miniature guitars. With his parents' permission, he selected a guitar, took his place in the band, and played away. A passing photographer caught the moment. What does that say about Lawson? Alert parents ask such questions. They also ask about . . .

Optimal conditions. Pine trees need different soil than oak trees. A cactus thrives in different conditions than a rosebush. What about the soil and the environment of your child? Some kids love to be noticed. Others prefer to hide in the crowd. Some relish deadlines. Others need ample preparation and help. Some do well taking tests. Others excel with the subject, but stumble through exams.

Rush Limbaugh made a D in public speaking, but today he relishes speaking into a radio microphone.[5] The West Point algebra entrance exam nearly excluded Omar Bradley from military life. He squeaked into the academy in the next-to-lowest group, but went on to earn the rank of a five-star general and oversee thousands of troops and millions of dollars in World War II.[6] We each have different optimal conditions. What are your children's?

Relationships. Before Golda Meir led Israel in the 1973 war, she led her fourth-grade class against Milwaukee public schools. She organized a protest to decry the inequity of requiring poor students to buy textbooks. At the age of eleven, she rented a hall, raised funds, and convinced her sister to recite a socialist poem in Yiddish, and then Meir addressed the assembly. Her mother urged her to write out her speech. The future Labor Party prime minister refused. "It made more sense to me just to say what I wanted to say."[7]

Like Golda, some are born to lead; others are born to follow. When it comes to relationships, what phrase best describes each of your children?

"Follow me, everyone."

"I'll let you know if I need some help."

"Can we do this together?"

"Tell me what to do, and I'll do it."

Don't characterize loners as aloof or crowd seekers as arrogant. They may be living out their story.

What gives your children satisfaction and pleasure? What makes them say, *"Yes!"* Do they love the journey or the goal? Do they like to keep things straight or straighten things out? What thrills one person bothers another. The apostle Peter liked to keep the boat steady while Paul was prone to rock it.

Strength. Topic. Optimal conditions. Relationships. Yes! You've been given a book with no title—read it! A CD with no cover—listen to it! An island with no owner—explore it! Resist the urge to label before you study. Attend carefully to the unique childhood of your child. What S.T.O.R.Y. do you read in your children? Uncommon are the parents who attempt to learn—and blessed are their children.

Childhood tendencies forecast adult abilities.

Read my name among the blessed. Crankcase oil coursed my dad's veins. He repaired oil-field engines for a living and rebuilt car engines for fun. He worked in grease and bolts like sculptors work in clay; they were his media of choice. Dad loved machines.

But God gave him a mechanical moron, a son who couldn't differentiate between a differential and a brake disc. My dad tried to teach me. I tried to learn. Honestly, I did. But more than once I actually dozed off under the car on which we were working. Machines anesthetized me. But books fascinated me. I biked to the library a thousand times. What does a mechanic do with a son who loves books?

He gives him a library card. Buys him a few volumes for Christmas. Places a lamp by his bed so he can read at night. Pays tuition so his son can study college literature in high school. My dad did that. You know what he didn't do? Never once did he say, "Why can't you be a mechanic like your dad and granddad?" Maybe he understood my bent. Or maybe he didn't want me to die of hunger. But somehow he knew to "train up a child in the way he should go."

God doesn't give parents manuscripts to write, but codes to decode. Study your kids while you can. The greatest gift you can give your children is not your riches, but revealing to them their own.

15

DON'T BE TOO BIG TO DO SOMETHING SMALL

As each one has received a special gift,
employ it in serving one another.

1 Peter 4:10 NASB

The view from Colorado's Mount Chrysolite steals what little breath the climb doesn't. A shawl of snow rests on the peaks to the east, marking the Continental Divide. You'd swear that's Montana you see to the north. Circles of ice-cold, trout-packed, pristine ponds stretch through the valley beneath you like a straight string of pearls.

Each Thursday during the summer some four hundred kids make the fourteen-thousand-foot climb. They've traveled from all over the nation to spend a week at Frontier Ranch, a Young Life camp. Some come to escape parents or hang out with a boyfriend. But before the week culminates, all hear about Jesus. And all will witness his work from the top of Mount Chrysolite.

They *all* will climb the peak. For that reason, several Young Life directors caboose the end of the pack. They prod and applaud, making sure every camper crests the top. I walked with them.

One young student, whose sweet spot shows great actuarial potential, counted the strides to the peak. Eight thousand. Somewhere around number four thousand Matthew from Minnesota[1] decided to call it quits, said he was too tired to take another step.

I took a quick liking to the guy. Most anyone would. Jovial. Pleasant and, in this case, donkey-determined not to climb that mountain. He let everyone but a few of us pass him. "I'm heading down," he announced. A Young Life staffer spelled out the consequences. "Can't send you down alone, friend. You turn back, we all turn back."

The small circle of "we," I realized, included "me." I didn't want to go back. I had two options: miss the mountaintop or help Matt see it.

I coaxed him, begged him, negotiated a plan with him. Thirty steps of walking. Sixty seconds of resting. We inched our way at this pace for an hour. Finally we stood within a thousand feet of the peak. But the last stretch of trail rose up as straight as a fireman's ladder.

God's cure for the common life includes a strong dose of servanthood.

We got serious. Two guys each took an arm, and I took the rear. I placed both hands on Matt's gluteus maximus and shoved. We all but dragged him past the timberline.

That's when we heard the applause. Four hundred kids on the crest of Mount Chrysolite gave Matt from Minnesota a standing ovation. They whooped and hollered and slapped him on the back.

As I slumped down to rest, this thought steamrolled my way. *There it is, Max, a picture of my plan. Do all you can to push each other to the top.* From God? Sounds like something he might say.

After all, his Son did that. Jesus's self-assigned purpose statement reads: "For even the Son of Man did not come to be served, but to serve, and to give His life a ransom for many" (Mark 10:45).

God's cure for the common life includes a strong dose of servanthood. Timely reminder. As you celebrate your unique design, be careful. Don't so focus on what you love to do that you neglect what needs to be done.

A 3:00 a.m. diaper change fits in very few sweet spots. Most S.T.O.R.Y.'s don't feature the strength of garage sweeping. Visiting your sick neighbor might not come naturally to you. Still, the sick need to be encouraged, garages need sweeping, and diapers need changing.

The world needs servants. People like Jesus, who "did not come to be served, but to serve." He chose remote Nazareth over center-stage Jerusalem, his dad's carpentry shop over a marble-columned palace, and three decades of anonymity over a life of popularity.

Jesus came to serve. He selected prayer over sleep, the wilderness over the Jordan, irascible apostles over obedient angels. I'd have gone with the angels. Given the choice, I would have built my apostle team out of cherubim and seraphim or Gabriel and Michael, eyewitnesses of Red Sea rescues and Mount Carmel falling fires. I'd choose the angels.

Not Jesus. He picked the people. Peter, Andrew, John, and Matthew. When they feared the storm, he stilled it. When they had no coin for taxes, he supplied it. And when they had no wine for the wedding or food for the multitude, he made both.

He came to serve.

He let a woman in Samaria interrupt his rest, a woman in adultery interrupt his sermon, a woman with a disease interrupt his plans, and one with remorse interrupt his meal.

Though none of the apostles washed his feet, he washed theirs. Though none of the soldiers at the cross begged for mercy, he extended it. And though his followers skedaddled like scared rabbits on Thursday, he came searching for them on Easter Sunday. The resurrected King ascended to heaven only after he'd spent forty days with his friends—teaching them, encouraging them . . . serving them.

Why? It's what he came to do. He came to serve.

Joseph Shulam, a Jerusalem pastor, tells a remarkable story of a man who simulated the actions of Jesus. The son of a rabbi battled severe emotional problems. One day the boy went into his backyard, removed all his clothing, assumed a crouched position, and began to gobble like a turkey. He did this, not just for hours or days, but for weeks. No pleading would dissuade him. No psychotherapist could help him.

A friend of the rabbi, having watched the boy and shared the father's grief, offered to help. He, too, went into the backyard and removed his clothes. He crouched beside the boy and began gobbling, turkeylike. For days, nothing changed. Finally the friend spoke to the son. "Do you think it would be all right for turkeys to wear shirts?" After some thought and many gobbles, the son agreed. So they put on their shirts.

Days later the friend asked the boy if it would be acceptable for turkeys to wear trousers. The boy nodded. In time, the friend redressed the boy. And, in time, the boy returned to normal.[2]

Do you find that story incredible? So do I. But not nearly as incredible as the actions of Jesus. He stripped himself of heaven's robe, layered himself in epidermis and hair, hunched down in our world, and spoke our language in the hope that he could lead this bunch of turkeys back home again. "He set aside the privileges of deity and took on the status of a slave, became *human*! Having become human, he stayed human. It was an incredibly humbling process. He didn't claim special privileges. Instead, he lived a selfless, obedient life and then died a selfless, obedient death—and the worst kind of death at that: a crucifixion" (Phil. 2:7–8 MSG).

Let's follow his example. Let's "put on the apron of humility, to serve one another" (1 Pet. 5:5 TEV). Jesus entered the world to serve. We can enter our jobs, our homes, our churches. Servanthood requires no unique skill or seminary degree. Regardless of your strengths, training, or church tenure, you can . . .

Love the overlooked. Jesus sits in your classroom, wearing the thick glasses, outdated clothing, and a sad face. You've seen him. He's Jesus.

Jesus works in your office. Pregnant again, she shows up to work late and tired. No one knows the father. According to water-cooler rumors, even she doesn't know the father. You've seen her. She's Jesus.

When you talk to the lonely student, befriend the weary mom, you love Jesus. He dresses in the garb of the overlooked and ignored. "Whenever you did one of these things to someone overlooked or ignored, that was me—you did it to me" (Matt. 25:40 MSG).

> Don't so focus
> on what you love
> to do that you
> neglect what
> needs to be done.

You can do that. Even if your sweet spot has nothing to do with encouraging others, the cure for the common life involves loving the overlooked.

You can also . . .

Wave a white flag. We fight so much. "Where do you think all these appalling wars and quarrels come from?" asks the brother of Jesus. "Do you think they just happen? Think again. They come about because you want your own way, and fight for it deep inside yourselves" (James 4:1 MSG).

Servants resist stubbornness. Ulrich Zwingli manifested such a spirit. He promoted unity during Europe's great Reformation. At one point he found himself at odds with Martin Luther. Zwingli did not know what to do. He found his answer one morning on the side of a Swiss mountain. He watched two goats traversing a narrow path from opposite directions, one ascending, the other descending. At one point the narrow trail prevented them from passing each other. When they saw each other, they backed up and lowered their heads, as though ready to lunge. But then a wonderful thing happened. The ascending goat lay down on the path. The other stepped over his back. The first animal then arose and continued his climb to the top. Zwingli observed that the goat made it higher because he was willing to bend lower.[3]

Didn't the same happen to Jesus? "So God raised him to the highest place. God made his name greater than every other name so that every knee will bow to the name of Jesus" (Phil. 2:9–10 NCV).

Serve someone by swallowing your pride. Regardless of your design, you can wave a white flag and . . .

Here is where the phone rang. At this point in the writing of this chapter, Denalyn called.

"Busy?" she asked.

"Sort of . . . Why?"

"I need help unloading a cooler."

"Oh . . ." My voice trailed.

"It's heavy. Can you come home and lift it out of the car?"

A cooler? I wanted to write, finish this point, craft a humanity-changing book, record words to bless future generations. *Does this woman not know my calling? Does she know to whom she is married?* Angels were taking notes over my shoulder. And she wanted me to come home and lift a cooler. I didn't want to help her.

And then I remembered the theme of the chapter. Ouch! Paul spoke to me when he wrote: "If you think you are too important to help someone in need, you are only fooling yourself. You are really a nobody" (Gal. 6:3 NLT).

> Servanthood requires no unique skill or seminary degree.

Denalyn's request revealed one more aspect of servanthood . . .

Every day do something you don't want to do. Pick up someone else's trash. Surrender your parking place. Call the long-winded relative. Carry the cooler. Doesn't have to be a big thing. Helen Keller once told the Tennessee legislature that when she was young, she had longed to do great things and could not, so she decided to do small things in a great way.[4] Don't be too big to do something small. "Throw yourselves into the work of the Master, confident that nothing you do for him is a waste of time or effort" (1 Cor. 15:58 MSG).

Baron de Rothschild once asked artist Ary Scheffer to paint his portrait. Though a wealthy financier, Rothschild posed as a beggar, wearing rags and holding a tin cup. During one day of painting, a friend of the artist entered the room. Thinking Rothschild was really a beggar, he dropped a coin in his cup.

Ten years later that man received a letter from Baron de Rothschild and a check for ten thousand francs. The message read, "You one day gave a coin to Baron de Rothschild in the studio of Ary Scheffer. He has invested it and today sends you the capital which you entrusted to him, together with the compounded interest. A good action always brings good fortune."[5]

We would add to that line. A good action not only brings good fortune, it brings God's attention. He notices the actions of servants. He sent his Son to be one.

When you and I crest Mount Zion and hear the applause of saints, we'll realize this: hands pushed us up the mountain too. The pierced hands of Jesus Christ, the greatest servant who ever lived.

Conclusion

Sweet Spots: Two People Who Found Theirs

You were chosen to tell about the excellent qualities of God.

1 Peter 2:9 GOD'S WORD

Ten-year-old Rich shudders beneath the sheets of his bed. His parents argue in the next room. Father drinking, again. Mother worrying, again. Never enough money. Never enough work. They yell and the boy trembles. Will they be thrown out of their house? Anxiety and anger fog the home. Rich remembers the decision of that cold night in Syracuse: "My parents can't help me. If I make it, I'll make it on my own."

In the seventh grade he requested and received catalogs from each of the Ivy League schools. Education, he resolved, would buy his bus ticket out of scarcity. College life led him to Cornell University, where scholarships paid the tuition, and hard work made the grades. He befriended others like him—students born, not with silver spoons, but iron anchors of misfortune. He recruited and led a ragtag volleyball team composed of players too short or inept to make the prestigious fraternity squads. Rich and his team won the university championship. Seems the poor boy from Syracuse had a soft spot for others like himself.

Good grades awarded him a scholarship to Wharton, where he earned an MBA and found the two loves of his life: Reneé and Jesus. Reneé suggested they register their wedding at the china section of a department store. Rich refused. "As long as there are hungry children, we shouldn't have china or crystal." The advocate for the underdog speaks again. At their wedding, Rich and Reneé received a closetful of fondue sets and Crock-Pots, but no china.

The business world came easily for Rich. By the age of thirty-three he occupied the CEO office of Parker Brothers, an international game and toy company. Eleven years later he'd changed companies and crested another corporate ladder, serving as the CEO of Lenox China and Crystal.

> When our gifts illuminate God and help his children, don't you think he beams!

Life was good: secure job, healthy family, nice home on five Pennsylvania acres. But something nagged at him. The irony of it all. The groom who had resisted the china registry was selling luxury goods and fine dinnerware to the wealthy.

Life seemed off balance. He knew *what* he did best—management. He knew *where* to do it—in large organizations. But *why*? He grew restless, considered early retirement. Move to Boca Raton and play golf. Reneé would have none of it. "If we retire, it will be to the mission field."

Mission field? Rich chuckled at the thought. He was no theologian, no agriculturist. What work of God needs a master of pro formas, budgets, and organizational charts?

World Vision did. The call came in 1998. *Would you consider assuming the role of CEO?* Rich had heard of the ministry, how they champion the cause of the poor worldwide. Rich knew what they did, but he had no clue why they wanted him. He declined the offer. World Vision persisted, convincing Rich to map out his life, assess his skills.

He reluctantly agreed, spending eight hours taking an expanded version of the resource that awaits you in the back of this book. The results convinced the World Vision board: Rich was made for the job.

Rich remained unconvinced. He saw the move as career suicide. Move his family from Pennsylvania to Seattle? Take a 75 percent pay cut? Assume the reins, not of a business, but a ministry? Most of all he feared failure. What if he blew it?

World Vision pressed him. Of the two hundred candidates, he was their choice. Board member Bill Hybels phoned and challenged Rich to make the jump. He spoke of sweet spots and eternal impacts. "This is a chance to marry your gifts with God's call. When you do that, you enter a zone— the zone in which you were made to live."

Rich Stearns prayed, weighed the options, and made the choice. He swapped porcelain sales for relief efforts, marketing meetings for strategy sessions on AIDS. Has he regretted it? Ask him and feel the energy pulsate through the phone. I barely wrote fast enough to capture his enthusiasm:

"This is the fulfillment of who I was created to be."

"I've found my stride."

"My work is *a thrill on blueberry hill.*"

"I wonder why I waited twenty-three years."

World Vision has no regrets either. In Rich's first six years, their annual budget more than doubled, jumping from $350 million to $807 million, making World Vision the largest relief organization in the history of the world.

Toward the end of our conversation, the kid from the troubled home quoted a favorite verse: "'I know the plans that I have for you,' declares the LORD, 'plans for welfare and not for calamity to give you a future and a hope'" (Jer. 29:11 NASB).

"Looking back," he says, "I can see the plan."

Can't we all? The underdog from Syracuse helps the underdogs of the world—and relishes every minute.[1]

o   o   o

Union University of Jackson, Tennessee, requires all freshmen to evaluate their strengths. Students do what this book urges you to do: string together pearls of success and celebration and wear the necklace.

They jump at the exercise. The question, what is your major? leaves many young people stuttering and shrugging. Nineteen-year-old Lori Neal was one of them. She needed some direction in life. *Do I go to medical school? Perhaps study business?* She was best known for sports, having played three in high school and earned a college softball scholarship. She assumed her S.T.O.R.Y. would reveal athletic strengths. She was in for a surprise. Glimpse at her assessment and see what you see.

One story described a miniature, doll-sized swimming pool she had dug in her backyard. Tinfoil-lined and waterfall-fed (through a water hose), it "was better than the real thing you buy at a store."

Another essay recounted a high-school interior-design project: *draw a house blueprint and decorate the interior.* The assignment consumed her thoughts for three days and most of the nights. She searched magazines, selected colors, chose furniture. "I never felt like I was working," she wrote. "I loved it."

One happy memory began as an antidote to summer boredom. She bought cake-decorating supplies and a how-to book and got to work. Not only did time pass, she made some money.

Digging a pool. Designing a house. Decorating a cake.

Where are the sports moments? she wondered. No mention of home runs (she hit many) or game-winning shots (she made some). Athletic ability took a backseat to creativity.

Lori tested the test. She dropped sophomore chemistry and business classes and signed up for two art courses. The subject amazed her. The art history class that heavied the eyelids of her friends popped hers wide open. On the final exam the teacher asked, "What did you learn from art history?" Lori wrote her answer in uppercase letters: "I AM AN ARTIST!"

> Don't see yourself as a product of your parents' DNA, but rather as a brand-new idea from heaven.

She dived into the university's art curriculum. Ceramics raced her pulse the most. More than once she looked up from her project to find the studio empty and the clock reading 4:00 a.m. At the school-sponsored ceramics sale, she sold everything. "I can make a living at this," she realized.

Within three years the confused, softball-playing freshman was a focused and recognized college senior. The prestigious *Ceramics Monthly* published her writings, and the world's premier ceramic school, Alfred University, invited her to study on their campus.

To catch up with Lori, I phoned Italy, where she continues her graduate studies. One request, "Tell me about your interest in art," prompted a forty-five-minute reply that bubbled with comments such as . . .

"I'm passionate about my work."

"I love what I do."

"I can spend my life doing this."

"God gave me talents as a gift to me. My gift to him is to use those talents to his glory."

"But how?" I asked. "How can your art career make a big deal out of God?"

She gave two answers. "The art world has few Jesus followers. When I do my best, they notice, not just me, but my Lord."

Her second response would warm the coldest heart. She described the feeling she had when she worked at a rehab center one summer. Among the chores she dreaded was one she cherished—drawing pictures on balloons and giving them to handicapped children. "When the work of my hands makes little girls smile, that's where my heart is."[2] Not a bad sweet spot: using the work of her hands to bring smiles to people's faces.

> A common life? Heaven knows no such phrase.

God smiles too. When our gifts illuminate him and help his children, don't you think he beams! Let's spend a lifetime making him proud.

Use your uniqueness to do so. You exited the womb called. Don't see yourself as a product of your parents' DNA, but rather as a brand-new idea from heaven.

Make a big deal out of God. Become who you are for him! Has he not transferred you from a dull, death-destined life to a rich, heaven-bound adventure? Remember, "you were chosen to tell about the excellent qualities of God" (1 Pet. 2:9 GOD'S WORD). And do so *every day of your life.*

A common life? Heaven knows no such phrase. With God, every day matters, every person counts.

And that includes you.

You do something no one else does, in a manner no one else does it. And when your uniqueness meets God's purpose, both of you will rejoice . . . forever.

SWEET SPOT
DISCOVERY GUIDE

by

People Management International, Inc.

and

Steve Halliday

THE CURE FOR
THE COMMON LIFE

You were born prepacked—for a purpose! Long before you were born, God equipped you with special and unique tools to achieve his purpose and fulfill his plan. Discovering what he gave you is the first step toward curing the common life.

This discovery guide will help you do just that. It features two distinct sections. My good friends at People Management International, Inc. have developed the first part of this guide, and I've called on curriculum specialist Steve Halliday to create the second part.

The first section is designed for personal use. It encourages you to reflect and expand on your personal success stories in order to explore the distinctive S.T.O.R.Y. God has written in your life.

Keep in mind that this first section is an *initial* exploration, designed to help you consider and identify your uniqueness and gifts. To find and enjoy your sweet spot, you have to thoroughly explore your S.T.O.R.Y. So remember, the following tool is just a beginning; if you would like to go deeper, other workbooks and resources are available.

We'll describe the second part of the study guide when we get to it. But for now, let's plunge in!

Part One

THE FIRST STEP TOWARD FINDING YOUR SWEET SPOT

It's time to look for your sweet spot—where *what* you do (your unique giftedness) intersects with *why* you do it (making a big deal out of God) and *where* you do it (every day of your life). How do you discover what God packed in your bag?

Simple: identify things you love to do that you also do well. Consider these your sweet spot experiences. Think of times of full-flight energy, of unclocked time. Times when you thought, *I was **made for this!*** Times when you felt a rush of accomplishment. You at your best. These foundational experiences reveal your uniqueness and help you identify your sweet spot.

To unlock their secrets, all you have to do is read your life backward.

The Process: Recall Your Sweet Spot Experiences

Take a trip down memory lane. Think about your whole life, starting in childhood. Recall times when you . . .

- did something well (success)
- and enjoyed doing it (satisfaction).

Remember, you find your sweet spot at the intersection of success and satisfaction. These sweet spot experiences are not merely pleasant times ("I love to listen to good music"); instead, they are times when you did something well that also gave you a feeling of accomplishment ("I collected and classified all the records and CDs made by Ray Charles"). Anything that gives you a sense of joy and achievement is important, no matter how trivial it may seem.

Also, keep in mind that these times must be important to *you*. What family or friends think is not so important right now.

Sweet spot experiences can occur in ten-minute periods or a day, a week, a summer, a year, several years, or even longer. You can draw sweet spot experiences from any part of your life: outside school, inside school, in your work, in leisure, in friends, in family—any segment of life.

People Management International Inc. has used the following process for the past forty-five years to identify the unique giftedness of thousands of men and women throughout the world in churches, industry, and education. While this tool will only get you started down the road to finding your sweet spot, you can be sure that God will use it to reveal much to you, as he already has to countless others.

Before you start identifying your sweet spot experiences, consider a few examples of sweet spot experiences that others have identified in their lives.

Youthful Sweet Spot Experiences

- Tried out for the high-school play, got a role, and overcame my stammer.

- In third grade I drew a "space car," and everyone wanted to know how.
- Turned my stereo into a radio station and broadcast to the neighborhood kids.
- Built a stereo set from a kit.
- Stood up for a slow learner who was being ridiculed.
- Invented my own computer game.
- Researched Mexican cuisine and cooked a four-course meal.
- Helped build a three-story tree house.
- Taught myself how to use watercolors.
- Tackled the runner ten yards from the goal line.
- I befriended a Russian girl who spoke no English.
- I increased my paper route to 150 customers.
- My sister and I imitated all the big stars.
- I supported my whole family for two years.
- I created an outfit that looked exactly like the one in the window.

Adult Sweet Spot Experiences

- I taught a young blind boy how to swim.
- Created a dining-room window treatment out of grapevine, fabric, twinkle lights, and fruit.
- Organized my children's building blocks by size and kind so they could access them better when they played.
- Built a seventy-ton boulder retaining wall in my backyard over two summers.

- Found my own apartment and furnished it for under $500.

- Won a long and difficult dispute with a large auto dealership.

- Designed and published a new fashion newsletter.

- Helped my daughter overcome a debilitating disease.

- Ran a program at church that made over $10,000 for charity.

- Smoothed over a labor-relations problem.

- Put in more than a hundred plants one spring.

- Designed and built a cabin, did major portion of the manual work.

- Tuned a piano with the aid of an electronic-frequency counter.

- Successfully led small unit through numerous missions in Vietnam.

- Stayed within $32 of operating budget, though work had doubled.

Please note that *all* these examples are

- specific events, not general activities;

- specific accomplishments, not significant milestones (such as getting married or divorced);

- specific actions ("I was good at Monopoly"), not generalities ("I loved to play sports").

One-Liners of Your Sweet Spot Experiences

Now start with your early childhood and recall something that you enjoyed doing and that you believe you did well. Proceed through the years, writing a one-liner for each of these experiences. What really gave you pleasure?

Enjoy yourself, and realize that your sweet spot experiences, as small and inconspicuous as they may seem, in fact begin to introduce you to who

God made you to be. Don't be shy or modest! Remember, this is God's plan. So "make a careful exploration of who you are" (Gal. 6:4 MSG).

Childhood

_____

_____

_____

_____

_____

Youth

_____

_____

_____

_____

_____

Adult

_____

_____

_____

_____

_____

Our next step will be to expand on these stories with more details, but before you do that, let's check out how others expanded on their sweet spot experiences.

Example #1 Summary:

Playing scrub baseball (I sometimes helped organize).

Details of how you went about doing it:

Sometimes I played at school and other times just got in on neighborhood games. One summer though, I asked, "Why not have a first-class team?" So I went around to kids I knew who were really good and asked them to play. I chose the name ("Blackhawks") and was co-captain with another friend (had to share that with him to get him to join up), but I assigned most of the positions. At the beginning I also set up most of the games. Would decide a few days in advance, phone around, and get others to phone—never did much to have a real schedule.

What felt most satisfying to you?

The chance to win.

Example #2 Summary:

I tutored a guy who had not passed the college-entrance test in math and saw him graduate as a math major.

Details of how you went about doing it:

I guess it all started when I saw him outside the lecture hall one Thursday; he looked a little glum, so I asked him, "What's wrong?" At first he said, "Nothing," but when he saw I really wanted to know, he told me he hadn't passed the math entrance exam and was in danger of not getting in. I asked him if I could help, and that's how we got started, with me helping him to understand the basics of math. It opened a whole new world to him. I used to make him explain to me just how he got the answer he did. I made myself constantly available to him.

What felt most satisfying to you?
Just to think that I helped someone to understand and helped him to do something he really enjoyed. . . . You feel like you've accomplished something that really helps someone.

Example #3 Summary:
Set up a daily pending file for my employer.

Details of how you went about doing it:
I set up a series of follow-up letters—some were forms, some dictated by the boss, and others I handled myself. I enjoyed taking dictation, then being left alone to work the final "product." There was a good variety of work: secretarial, posting, payroll reconciling statements, making department spreadsheets. I liked working with figures and details and enjoyed going to work, knowing what I had to do and doing it. The pending file itself was my idea to work out. It was a good follow-up that allowed me to check up and make sure things got done and were not lost in the shuffle.

What felt most satisfying to you?
I could handle every aspect of the work.

It's Your Turn

Now start writing *your* S.T.O.R.Y. just as you might tell a friend about what you did. Pick four to six of your sweet spot experience one-liners that feel significant to you. Expand on them by describing action details—everything you remember doing that helped you to accomplish your goal. Concentrate on what you were good at doing. Don't generalize; be specific. Use examples or illustrations of what you did. Pretend you are revisiting the scene or situations and observing yourself as you performed the tasks. Be generous in writing what happened, but stick to *specific* actions. Start in your childhood or youth and work forward.

Summary:

_____

_____

_____

_____

_____

_____

Details of how you went about doing it:

_____

_____

_____

_____

_____

_____

What felt most satisfying to you?

_____

_____

_____

_____

_____

Summary:

_____

_____

_____

_____

_____

_____

Details of how you went about doing it:

_____

_____

_____

_____

What felt most satisfying to you?

_____

_____

_____

_____

Summary:

_____
_____
_____
_____

_____
_____
_____
_____

Details of how you went about doing it:

_____
_____
_____
_____
_____
_____

What felt most satisfying to you?

_____
_____
_____
_____
_____
_____

Summary:

_____

_____

_____

_____

_____

_____

_____

_____

Details of how you went about doing it:

_____

_____

_____

_____

_____

_____

_____

What felt most satisfying to you?

_____

_____

_____

_____

_____

_____

Summary:

_____

_____

_____

_____

_____

_____

_____

Details of how you went about doing it:

_____

_____

_____

_____

_____

_____

_____

What felt most satisfying to you?

_____

_____

_____

_____

_____

_____

_____

Summary:

_____

_____

_____

_____

_____

_____

_____

_____

Details of how you went about doing it:

_____

_____

_____

_____

_____

_____

What felt most satisfying to you?

_____

_____

_____

_____

_____

Identifying the Recurring Themes in Your Life

Whenever you do something you enjoy and believe you do well, you're using some or all of the elements of your giftedness. When you read your life backward by recalling a lifetime of sweet spot experiences, you can begin to see certain recurring themes, such as

- how you learn or practice a skill;
- how you evaluate whether to spend money on something;
- how you decide to take a risk;
- how you set a goal or develop a strategy;
- how you put ingredients together exactly or casually.

You may find recurring themes in how you always seem to be fixing mechanical things; how you tend to get involved with a group or with people one-on-one; how you love words and stories or foreign languages; how you spend much of your time collecting stamps or coins or baseball cards; how you worry about all the details of running the prom, the wedding, or the conference; how you enjoy working out, biking, building stone walls or tree houses, shooting buckets, or running marathons.

You get the idea.

Ask yourself some questions. Do others always ask for your help or invite you to join in? Are you careful to organize everything you do? Does it seem that you're always onstage or getting some kind of recognition? Are you a constant competitor, always keeping score? Do you like working with a team or group, or do you find the role of an individualist more enjoyable? Do you like to be at the center of things and coordinate others? Did you begin leading your friends at age six and have never stopped?

Such recurring themes indicate where your sweet spot may lie.

Let's see if we can spot the themes in the following story examples from Marie, who is starting to uncover her sweet spot. She is aware that her current work isn't using her uniqueness, so she wants to look more closely at how God designed her. Let's search for themes in her sweet spot experiences that mark her giftedness. Highlight or circle what you see recurring in these stories, and write those after the last story.

Childhood one-line summary:
Led the crossing-guard patrol in grade school.

Details of how you went about doing it:
It was my responsibility to make sure the schedule was organized and that the kids had all of the stations around the school covered before and after school. I weeded out some of the more unreliable kids and replaced them with other kids I recruited to help. During our times on duty, I'd tour around to make sure everything was going well and help or direct the kids when needed.

What felt most satisfying to you?
We didn't have any accidents, and the whole safety patrol worked better than it ever had before.

College one-line summary:
Helped make living in the dorms better for freshmen and sophomores.

Details of how you went about doing it:

I initiated group meetings at our dorm to find out student needs. I appointed dorm captains for each of the four floors and organized groups to address the various needs for the under-classmen. Coping with college life and getting around was tough for them, so I coordinated two of the captains to provide ongoing orientation to the campus. I put the other two in charge of the monthly all-dorm meeting facilitation. I would watch over all the activity of the dorm and have weekly meetings with the four captains to help and keep them on track. I would assign people special tasks as the need came up.

What felt most satisfying to you?

We were able to improve the dorm experience students had in their first year of college.

Adult one-line summary:

Led the neighborhood association for two years.

Details of how you went about doing it:

After I got elected to the role, I knocked on doors of the neighbors I didn't know very well to introduce myself. I'd size up each person to see if they might want to do special projects around the area by asking them questions. Our neighborhood park was getting a little shabby, so I called up six people who wanted to get involved and asked them to be on the park-improvement team. I picked the day and time and came up with a to-do list and assigned people work they thought would be most fun. I picked a job too (rearranging the gazebo furniture), while answering questions and helping people stay on task. Later I organized a party in the park, and everybody was blown away with our work!

What felt most satisfying to you?

The park looked great—cleaner and more pleasant—and I enjoyed seeing people relate to each other better than they had before.

As you attempt to identify some of the themes revealed in Marie's sweet spot experiences, begin by looking at your overall impression or picture of her. Notice how she responds to situations where needs present themselves (underline those words and phrases). See how she is always organizing and coordinating (underline those themes). Check out how she focuses on the logistics and the people (underline). Finally, look at what is most satisfying to her—she's always improving situations!

While it's necessary to identify recurring themes, we need to go deeper than that. The elements that recur in an individual's achievements tend to fall into the following five categories.

S = Strengths: how you get things done using your unique gifts. The verbs you use to describe your activities reveal these strengths.

T = Topics: what you want to work with. You feel completely absorbed when you get involved in this, whatever it is—be it a person, a group, a car, a concept, food, music, fabric, furniture, or anything else in God's creation. The nouns you use reveal these topics.

O = Optimal conditions: the conditions in our environments that make things best for us. For example, some people work best under pressure; some need challenges; some like structure; some like an audience. What triggers you, gets you started, sustains your drive, defines the tasks, and provides the setting for you to feel highly motivated to effectively accomplish the task is part of your optimal conditions.

R = Relationships: what kind of role and relationship to others you seek in the task.

Y = Yes! You achieve this joyous affirmation when you fulfill the purpose for which you were designed. At that moment your sweet spot experience tastes ever so sweet!

Before you try to identify your particular gift mix, let's see an example of how this works. Following are the three stories from Marie. We are now going to look at them through the S.T.O.R.Y. framework. Note that in the stories, verbs are underlined (her Strengths), and nouns are boxed (her Topics). We will pull all of Marie's S.T.O.R.Y. components together in a chart on page 167. This chart will give you a framework for identifying your gift mix in your stories.

Childhood one-line summary:
Led the crossing-guard patrol in grade school.

Details of how you went about doing it:

It was my responsibility to make sure the schedule was organized and that the kids had all of the stations around the school covered before and after school. I weeded out some of the more unreliable kids and replaced them with other kids I recruited to help. During our times on duty, I'd tour around to make sure everything was going well and help or direct the kids when needed.

What felt most satisfying to you?

We didn't have any accidents, and the whole safety patrol worked better than it ever had before.

College one-line summary:

Helped make living in the dorms better for freshmen and sophomores.

Details of how you went about doing it:

I initiated group meetings at our dorm to find out student needs. I appointed dorm captains for each of the four floors and organized groups to address the various needs for the underclassmen. Coping with college life and getting around was tough for them, so I coordinated two of the captains to provide ongoing orientation to the campus. I put the other two in charge of the monthly all-dorm meeting facilitation. I would watch over all the activity of the dorm and have weekly meetings with the four captains to help and keep them on track. I would assign people special tasks as the need came up.

What felt most satisfying to you?

We were able to improve the dorm experience students had in their first year of college.

Adult one-line summary:

Led the neighborhood association for two years.

Details of how you went about doing it:

After I got elected to the role, I knocked on doors of the neighbors I didn't know very well to introduce myself. I'd size up each person to see if they might want to do special projects around the area by asking them questions. Our neighborhood park was getting a little shabby, so I called up six people who wanted to get involved and asked them to be on the park-improvement team. I picked the day and time and came up with a to-do list and assigned people work they thought would be most fun. I picked a job too (rearranging the gazebo furniture), while answering questions and helping people stay on task. Later I organized a party in the park, and everybody was blown away with our work!

What felt most satisfying to you?
The park looked great—cleaner and more pleasant—and I enjoyed seeing people relate to each other better than they had before.

This story chart is where Marie collected the most important recurring S.T.O.R.Y. elements and statements from her sweet spot experiences. Looking at all her stories, she filled in the chart with her Strengths, Topics, Optimal conditions, Relationships, and her Yes! She is beginning to see some themes!

Strengths: (List the underlined verbs and actions from your stories.)	make sure; organized; weeded out; replaced; recruited; tour around; help; direct; initiated; find out; appointed; coordinated; put the other two in charge; watch over; help and keep them on track; assign; introduce; size up; asking them; called up; picked; came up with; answering
Topics: (List the boxed nouns and subjects from your stories.)	group meetings; student needs; dorm captains; groups; all the activity; weekly meetings; people; special tasks; schedule; kids; day and time; to-do list; party
Optimal conditions: (Describe what gets your energy started and keeps you going in your stories.)	I responded to needs; liked conditions that needed structure to make them better.
Relationships: (In your own words describe what role and relationship to others you take on in your stories.)	exercised initiative; coordinated and supervised others
Yes! (Describe what themes you see in "What felt most satisfying to you?")	made things better! improved the situation!

Pulling All the Pieces Together

You can easily see how all the pieces work together in a person's life if you put them in a statement that links them to the Yes! component (what he or she is created to achieve). Take Marie, whose sweet spot experiences you just considered. The following paragraph shows how all the pieces in her S.T.O.R.Y. work together to help accomplish her Yes! You'll have a chance to do this for yourself in a few pages.

Marie's S.T.O.R.Y.

The themes in my S.T.O.R.Y. show that God has put me together so that I love to (S) initiate change, organize people, watch over what's happening, assign tasks, and recruit and direct others. I particularly like to do that with (T) schedules, to-do lists, meetings, and people in groups and communities. I work best in conditions (O) that need change, structure, and order, and I am at my best when I'm in the role of a (R) coordinator who initiates and supervises others. All of these elements of my S.T.O.R.Y. work together so that I can (Y) improve things and affect others.

The Difference This Makes!

Remember the stories that Marie told. She was most satisfied and joy filled when she was leading the crossing guards, coordinating the dorm captains, and organizing the neighborhood association. Yet, like many people, Marie finds that her life has become more and more unfulfilling. She works alone in the back office of a small company, inputting inventory data into the computer system. Every day is the same. What is the cure for this common life? First she needed to unpack her bags and uncover the tools God had given her. Reading her life backward, she can now see how God put her together. This helps her understand her frustration. In her current role she is not using her gifts or uniqueness!

She realizes she is most joyful when she can oversee others in a team and bring about change and improvement. No wonder she dreads her job. Knowing her pattern helps her realize that her best (to give to God) is to be in a role where she can manage others toward change. Her current job has her working alone and doing the same thing day in and day out. God created her to be a change agent of people and groups. This is part of his special purpose for her on this earth. She now can be more intentional about her choices for her next role.

Story Chart

This chart is a place for you to write in your important recurring elements and statements from your stories, just as Marie did.

Strengths: (List the underlined verbs and actions from your stories.)	
Topics: (List the boxed nouns and subjects from your stories.)	
Optimal conditions: (Describe what gets your energy started and keeps you going in your stories.)	
Relationships: (Describe what role and relationship to others you take on in your stories.)	
Yes! (Describe what themes you see in "What felt most satisfying to you?")	

Putting Together Your S.T.O.R.Y.

Use the following to crystallize what you have learned about your gift mix:

The themes in my S.T.O.R.Y. show that God has put me together so that I love to (insert your **Strengths**)

_____

_____

I particularly like to do that with (insert your **Topics**)

_____

_____

I work best in optimal conditions that include (insert your **Optimal** conditions)

_____

_____

And I am at my best when I'm in the role of (insert your **Relationships**)

_____

_____

All these themes of my S.T.O.R.Y. work together so that I can (insert your **Yes!**)

_____

_____

A Sweet Discovery!

Think about the previous statements for a moment. Are you beginning to notice a theme in your sweet spot stories? In this theme you can begin to discover what God has purposed for your life. God created you for joy-filled, fruitful service. There is a pattern in your joy! Your themes reveal your unique gift mix. You really are on track to discover what God wants you to do with your life. You are well on the road to discovering your own sweet spot!

Remember, God has designed you and gifted you in a unique way so you can fulfill the special purpose he has in mind just for you. As you increasingly understand your giftedness, you can build your life, your work, and your ministry on God's unique will for *you*.

But as you learned in *Cure for the Common Life*, finding your sweet spot takes more than just discovering your unique gift mix. That's a crucial step, but it's only the first step. To find your sweet spot, you must:

use your uniqueness (what you do)

> **to make a big deal out of God** (why you do it)

>> **every day of your life** (where you do it).

That brings us to part 2 of the study guide.

Part Two

NEXT STEPS TO FINDING YOUR SWEET SPOT

Now that you have a much better idea of your unique gift mix (what you do), you're ready to start exploring how you can make a big deal out of God every day of your life.

This second section of the study guide may be used by you individually or in a group discussion. It works hand in hand with sections 2 and 3 of *Cure for the Common Life* ("To Make a Big Deal Out of God" and "Every Day of Your Life"). The study questions that follow focus on three areas:

- *Review the Diagnosis:* questions to help you interact with the main point of each chapter
- *Respect the Prescription:* questions to help you interact with key Scripture passages on the topic of discussion

- *Reawaken the Excitement:* application sections to help you integrate what you discovered in your S.T.O.R.Y. with the main focus of each chapter in order to bring passion and excitement to your life of faith

Remember, your God-given gifts enable you to do something in a manner that no one else can. And when you find it and do it, you're living in your sweet spot.

TAKE BIG RISKS FOR GOD

Cure for the Common Life: Chapter 6

Review the Diagnosis

1. How you relate to the master of the house colors everything. Dread him and hate your work. Trust him and love it.

   A. Who is the master of *your* house? Explain.

   B. Do you see your work as a kingdom assignment? If so, in what way?

   C. How do you trust your master on a day-to-day basis? How do you demonstrate your trust?

2. The only mistake is not to risk making one. Such was the error of the one-talent servant.

   A. What kind of risks have you taken for God?

   B. What keeps you from taking risks for God?

   C. How has God shown himself faithful in the risks you have taken for him?

3. The first two invested. The last one buried. The first two went out on a limb. The third hugged the trunk. He made the most tragic and common mistake of giftedness. He failed to benefit the master with his talent.

   A. How are you investing your talents for the Lord?

   B. In what areas might you be "burying" your talent or "hugging the trunk"?

   C. Are there talents you're using—but not for the Lord's benefit? Explain.

4. The master repeated the assessment of the servant, word for word, with one exclusion. Did you note it? "I knew you to be a hard man." The master didn't repeat the description he wouldn't accept.

   A. What causes some people to think of God as a "hard" master?

   B. Why won't Jesus accept a description of his Father as "hard"?

   C. When people think of God as a hard master, how do they normally react?

5. Who is this unprofitable servant? If you never use your gifts for God, you are. If you think God is a hard God, you are. And you will live a life of interred talents.

   A. On a scale of 1 to 10, with 1 being unprofitable and 10 being profitable, how would you rate yourself? Explain.

   B. Have you ever thought of God as a hard God? What were the circumstances?

   C. Which gift could you use more fully for God? What steps could you take to begin "investing" it for him?

Respect the Prescription

1. Read Matthew 25:14–30.

   A. To which of the three servants portrayed in this parable do you most relate? Why?

   B. How does the master respond to each of the three servants in this parable?

   C. What general principle does Jesus outline in verse 29? How do you personally react to this principle? Explain.

2. Read Psalm 103:8–13.

   A. How is God described in verse 8? Have you experienced God in this way? Explain.

   B. What is the main point of verse 12?

   C. To what does the psalmist compare God in verse 13? Why is this important?

3. Read 2 Corinthians 11:24–28 and Philippians 4:12–13.

   A. How did the apostle Paul risk his life for Christ?

   B. What do you think prompted him to take life-endangering risks for God? According to Philippians, what was Paul's source of strength?

   C. How much are you willing to risk for God?

Reawaken the Excitement

1. What major personal Strength did you identify in your S.T.O.R.Y.? Spend a couple of days in prayer, asking God how you might use that strength in taking a risk for him. Once a clear idea of the risk you can take has formed in your mind, launch out and take the risk. Afterward, "debrief" with some mature Christian friends and discuss what happened. What did you learn? How can you use this experience to shape further risks you could take for God?

2. Read a biography of a courageous Christian who regularly took risks for God, such as William Carey, Amy Carmichael, George Müller, or Fannie Crosby. How can their examples embolden your enthusiasm for taking risks for God?

COME TO THE SWEETEST
SPOT IN THE UNIVERSE

Cure for the Common Life: Chapter 7

Review the Diagnosis

1. We may relish moments of solitude—but a lifetime of it? No way.

   A. Do you relish moments of solitude? Why or why not?

   B. Would you like a lifetime of solitude? Explain.

   C. Why do you think God created us to need other people?

2. *No one knows me. No one's near me. No one needs me.* How do you cope with such cries for significance?

   A. In your life, who knows you?

   B. In your life, who's near you?

   C. In your life, who needs you?

3. For thousands of years, God gave us his voice. Prior to Bethlehem, he gave his messengers, his teachers, his words. But in the manger, God gave us himself.

    A. For you, what's the main difference between God's giving us his voice and giving us himself?

    B. Why was it crucial for God to give us himself?

    C. How would your life be different if God had not given us himself?

4. The lonely heart of Giorgio Angelozzi drove him to look for a home. He found one. Unfortunately, his home won't last forever. But yours will.

    A. Where do you expect to spend eternity? Why?

    B. What do you expect your eternal home to be like?

    C. What would you say to others to explain how they can secure an eternal home with God?

5. Lonely? God is with you. Depleted? He funds the overdrawn. Weary of an ordinary existence? Your spiritual adventure awaits. The cure for the common life begins and ends with God.

    A. How does God help you overcome moments of loneliness?

    B. How does God refresh you and give you new strength when you feel weak?

    C. How has God put adventure into your life?

Respect the Prescription

1. Read 1 Peter 3:18.

   A. Why is it important that Christ died for sins "once for all" (NIV)?

   B. How does this verse describe Christ? How does it describe those for whom he died? Why is this contrast important to remember?

   C. How does Christ's death affect you personally?

2. Read John 12:27–32.

   A. Why was Jesus's heart troubled? What did he refuse to do about this troubled heart? Why (v. 27)?

   B. What would Jesus accomplish through his death, according to verse 31?

   C. What was Jesus's primary purpose in dying, according to verse 32?

3. Read Romans 5:6–8.

   A. What condition were we in when Christ died for us (v. 6)?

   B. What would have happened to us if God's attitude had been the same as people's attitude (v. 7)?

   C. What does the death of Christ prove about God's attitude toward us (v. 8)?

Reawaken the Excitement

1. Explain how your faith in Christ developed. In your spiritual journey, have any of your Strengths come into play? Which, if any, common Topics has God used? Has he placed you in any Optimal conditions

for your faith to grow? What **Relationships** has he used? How do you daily say **Yes!** to him?

2. Your personal testimony can help you share with someone who doesn't have a growing relationship with Christ. Use your S.T.O.R.Y. to talk naturally with him or her about Christ.

Applaud God, Loud and Often

Cure for the Common Life: Chapter 8

Review the Diagnosis

1. Neither omnipotent nor impotent, neither God's MVP nor God's mistake. Not self-secure or insecure, but God-secure—a self-worth based in our identity as children of God. The proper view of self is in the middle.

   A. Do you tend to think of yourself more as omnipotent or impotent? Explain.

   B. What does it mean to be "God-secure"?

   C. How would you describe your identity as a child of God?

2. Worship places God on center stage and us in proper posture.

   A. How would you describe worship?

   B. How does worship place God on center stage?

   C. How does worship place us in proper posture? What is this proper posture?

3. Worship humbles the smug. By the same token, worship lifts the deflated.

   A. Think of a worship moment in which you felt humbled. What happened?

   B. How does worship lift the deflated?

   C. What worship songs or moments lift you when you're deflated?

4. Cure any flareup of commonness by setting your eyes on our uncommon King.

   A. In what ways is our King uncommon?

   B. How do you set your eyes on our King?

   C. What happens when you set your eyes on our King?

5. Worship God. Applaud him loud and often. For your sake, you need it. And for heaven's sake, he deserves it.

   A. How important is worship in your life? How do you demonstrate this importance?

   B. What does it mean to applaud God? How do you best do this?

   C. Why do you need worship? Why does God deserve worship?

Respect the Prescription

1. Read Psalm 29:1–2.

   A. What does "glory" mean to you? What does it mean to ascribe glory to God?

   B. Why is glory *due* to God?

   C. How would you describe God's holiness? What does it mean that God is holy?

2. Read Romans 12:1.

   A. To what does the "therefore" refer in this verse? How does what went before supply a reason for the command?

   B. How do *you* offer your body to God as a living sacrifice?

   C. How can you worship God through the proper use of your body?

3. Read John 4:21–24.

   A. Is geographical location crucial for a genuine experience of worship? Explain.

   B. In what way is salvation from the Jews?

   C. Why does God seek worshipers? What kind of worshipers does he seek?

Reawaken the Excitement

1. Think of the Topics part of your S.T.O.R.Y. What things do you personally prefer to work on? Take some time to brainstorm how you can more consciously worship God through working with those things. What can you do that you haven't done? What can you stop doing that keeps you from worshiping him in that area? This next week determine to consciously and joyfully worship God in that area. Keep a small journal of what happens. Then at the end of the week, read over your journal and thank God for what he's teaching you and how he's blessing you.

2. Get out a concordance and look up the word "worship." In what ways did the people of the Bible worship God? What activities are often associated with worship? How does what you find in the Bible square with your own experience?

JOIN GOD'S FAMILY OF FRIENDS

Cure for the Common Life: Chapter 9

Review the Diagnosis

1. God . . . offers you a family of friends and friends who are family—his church.

   A. What do you normally think of when "church" comes to mind?

   B. Why would God picture the church as his family?

   C. How connected are you to your church family?

2. An awkward but accurate translation of the verse might be "Have a friend/family devotion to each other in a friend/family sort of way." If Paul doesn't get us with the first adjective, he catches us with the second. In both he reminds us: the church is God's family.

   A. What traits of a family would describe your relationship to your church? Explain.

   B. How do you try to make others feel welcome in God's family?

C. Would you use the word "devotion" to describe your connection to your church? Explain.

3. Some people enjoy the shade of the church while refusing to set down any roots. God, yes. Church, no. They like the benefits, but resist commitment.

A. What's wrong with trying to divorce church from God?

B. What do you see as the benefits of church?

C. Why would someone resist committing to a local church?

4. Broken people . . . limp in on fractured faith, and if the church operates as the church, they find healing. Pastor-teachers touch and teach. Gospel bearers share good news. Prophets speak words of truth. Visionaries dream of greater impact. Some administer. Some pray. Some lead. Some follow. But all help to heal brokenness.

A. How have you found healing in the church?

B. How have you helped to heal someone else in the church?

C. Where would you say you fit in the church? How do you best serve God through the church?

5. God heals his family through his family. In the church we use our gifts to love each other, honor one another, keep an eye on troublemakers, and carry each other's burdens.

A. Why do you think God would choose to heal his family through his family?

B. How would you describe God's opinion of the church?

C. How are you actively loving others in the church?

Respect the Prescription

1. Read Ephesians 3:14–19.

   A. What "family" does Paul have in mind in verses 14–15?

   B. What are the pieces of Paul's prayer in verses 16–19?

   C. To what degree has Paul's prayer been fulfilled in your life?

2. Read Romans 12:10.

   A. How are you "devoted" to others in the church?

   B. How do you honor others in the church above yourself?

   C. Would you describe your church as a place of brotherly love? Explain.

3. Read James 5:16.

   A. What command does this verse give?

   B. What promise does this verse give?

   C. How is the church crucial to both the command and the promise?

Reawaken the Excitement

1. Meditate on the Relationships component of your S.T.O.R.Y. What ministries or groups at church best fit the way you prefer to relate to others? If you're a natural performer, maybe it's the drama group. If you love to meet new people, maybe it's the outreach committee. Identify two or three groups or individuals in your church with whom you think you have a natural affinity, and inquire this week

about your possible involvement in some new service opportunity. Explore the possibilities, and then try out at least one of them in the next month.

2. Spend a month visiting different types of religious groups and meetings. Explore what makes them unique. Ask regular attendees what they like about the group.

Tank Your Reputation

Cure for the Common Life: Chapter 10

Review the Diagnosis

1. I went off to college and heard a professor describe a Christ I'd never seen. A people-loving and death-defeating Christ. A Jesus who made time for the lonely, the losers . . . a Jesus who died for hypocrites like me. So I signed up. As much as I could, I gave him my heart.

   A. Describe the Christ you're used to seeing. What is he like?

   B. What does Max mean that he gave Jesus his heart, "as much as I could"?

   C. Have you given Jesus your heart? Explain.

2. One can't, at once, promote two reputations. Promote God's and forget yours. Or promote yours and forget God's. We must choose.

   A. Why can't someone promote two reputations at once?

   B. How do you promote God's reputation?

C. What usually prompts you to choose one of these reputations over the other?

3. Joseph tanked his reputation. He swapped his *tsadiq* diploma for a pregnant fiancée and an illegitimate son and made the big decision of discipleship. He placed God's plan ahead of his own. Would you be willing to do the same?

   A. How did placing God's plan ahead of his own cost Joseph his reputation?

   B. Do you think your plan for your life might conflict with God's plan? Explain.

   C. Are you willing to place God's plan ahead of your own? Why or why not?

4. You can protect your reputation or protect his. You have a choice.

   A. How do we often try to protect our reputations?

   B. Have you ever had to choose between protecting your reputation and his? Explain what happened.

   C. What was the short-term effect of your choice? What were the long-term effects?

5. God hunts for . . . Josephs through whom he can deliver Christ into the world.

   A. What qualities made Joseph a good candidate to serve as Jesus's foster father?

   B. Do you have any of these qualities? Explain.

   C. How might God want to "deliver Christ into the world" through you?

Respect the Prescription

1. Read Philippians 2:4–11.

   A. What connection do you see between verses 4 and 5?

   B. What guidance does Paul give us in verse 5?

   C. What single word would you use to describe Christ's attitude as outlined in verses 6–11?

2. Read Matthew 16:24–25.

   A. What does it mean to come after Jesus? What does this require?

   B. How do we try to save our own lives? What is the result?

   C. How does Jesus instruct us to lose our lives? What is the result?

3. Read Proverbs 29:25.

   A. What warning does this verse give?

   B. What reassurance does this verse give?

   C. How can you heed the advice of this verse in your own life? At work? In your community?

Reawaken the Excitement

1. Think of the Yes! portion of your S.T.O.R.Y. Does the idea of making a big deal out of God drive you or motivate you in some way? If so, how? Look ahead to next week. What single event or job or task will probably consume most of your time? Does it incorporate your Yes!? What can you do in that event or job or task that will make a big deal out of God? How can you perform that activity in a way that emphasizes God's reputation and not your own?

2. Imagine that God had picked you to be the earthly "foster parent" of Jesus. What would make you a good candidate for the job? What personal qualities would likely give you trouble? Make a list of both your perceived strengths and weaknesses as the person whom God gave the job of raising his Son. What do these lists suggest about the areas where you might need help?

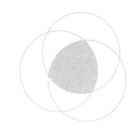

TAKE YOUR JOB
AND LOVE IT

Cure for the Common Life: Chapter 11

Review the Diagnosis

1. Two workers. One pumped up. One worn-out. The first, fruitful. The second, futile. To which do you relate?

   A. Would you describe yourself as more pumped up or worn-out at your job? Explain.

   B. Do you feel more fruitful or futile at your job? Explain.

   C. What do you think keeps you from feeling more pumped up and fruitful at your job?

2. God's eyes fall on the work of our hands. Our Wednesdays matter to him as much as our Sundays. He blurs the secular and sacred.

   A. Do you think God cares about your work? Explain.

   B. How does God blur the secular and the sacred?

   C. Do you blur the secular and the sacred? Explain.

3. Suppose you were to do what Peter did. Take Christ to work with you. Invite him to superintend your nine-to-five.

   A. How would you restructure your workday, guided by this premise?

   B. What challenges would you face if you took this course of action?

   C. What kind of job review would you get from Christ if he sat down with you today to give you one?

4. God can make a garden out of the cesspool you call work, if you take him with you.

   A. Would you describe your job as more like a garden or a cesspool? Explain.

   B. How do you think God could improve your attitude toward your work?

   C. If you were to take God with you to work, what things do you think would change first?

5. Everything changes when you give Jesus your boat.

   A. Think of specific changes that would occur in your relationships with co-workers if you were to "give Jesus your boat."

   B. Do you resist giving Jesus your boat? Explain.

   C. What promise does Jesus give you if you will give him your boat?

Respect the Prescription

1. Read Luke 5:1–11.

   A. Why do you think Peter told Jesus of his objection to his instructions, before he complied (v. 5)?

    B. Why do you think Peter responded as he did in verse 8?

    C. What promise did Jesus give Peter in verse 10?

2. Read Colossians 3:23–24.

    A. For whom do we really work, according to verse 23?

    B. How is this change of perspective supposed to affect the way we work?

    C. What promise is given in verse 24 that motivates us to follow the instruction of verse 23?

3. Read Psalm 90:17.

    A. What blessing does Moses ask for here? Have you asked for this blessing? Why or why not?

    B. What request does Moses make two times? Why does he ask twice?

    C. Do you believe that God is involved in the success of your work? Why or why not?

Reawaken the Excitement

1. Review the results for the Optimal-conditions portion of your S.T.O.R.Y.—the "where" and "when" you most like working. Does your current job seem to match these optimal conditions? If not, how close does it come? What could you do, if anything, to make your work conditions more closely match these optimal conditions? Can you talk to your boss or supervisor about it? Can you take certain actions on your own? You can certainly talk to the Lord about it. Make this a focus of your prayer life for the next week. Ask the Lord

to help you become more effective and fulfilled in your work and to remind you daily that you really work for him. If you have not already done so, give him your work life—and be willing to make a change if that is how he leads.

2. Write out the words of Colossians 3:17 or Colossians 3:22–24 on a small index card and take it to work. Keep it in your pocket or place it on your desk or at your work station, and read it several times a day to remind you of the truth. After a week, evaluate how your attitude toward work might be changing.

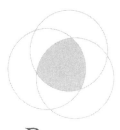

PAUSE
ON PURPOSE

Cure for the Common Life: Chapter 12

Review the Diagnosis

1. The two players had stepped away from the game. How long since you did the same? To stay sweet spot centered you must. The devil is determined to bump you out of your strengths. We need regular recalibrations.

   A. How long has it been since you "stepped away from the game"?

   B. In what areas of your life are you most likely to get bumped out of your strengths?

   C. How do you get recalibrated? How often do you intentionally get recalibrated?

2. Jesus baffled the public-relations experts by placing the mob in the rearview mirror and ducking into a wildlife preserve, a hidden cove, a vacant building, a *deserted place.*

A. Why do you think Jesus regularly got away from the crowds who needed him?

B. Why would Jesus choose to go to a deserted place?

C. If your circumstances do not permit a literal escape, how can you create a "deserted place" where you are?

3. I exist to reflect God through clear teaching and compelling stories. He then asked the question that undid me. "Does your calendar reflect your passion?"

A. Why do you exist? What single sentence describes your mission in life?

B. Does your calendar reflect your passion?

C. If your calendar doesn't reflect your passion, what can you do, starting today, to change things?

4. I now own a walking stick and a wide-brimmed hat. A favorite trail in a nearby nature park knows the feel of my steps. I'm a remedial student in the course of pausing, but my grades are improving.

A. What is the promise in "pausing"?

B. Are your grades improving in "the course of pausing"?

C. What most often keeps you from pausing as you know you should?

5. Follow Jesus into the desert. A thousand and one voices will scream like banana-tree monkeys telling you not to. Ignore them. Heed him.

A. Where is your "desert"? Why did you choose it?

B. Who is most likely to scream like a banana-tree monkey, urging you not to follow Jesus?

C. What can you do to make it more likely you'll heed Jesus and ignore the screamers?

Respect the Prescription

1. Read Mark 6:30–32.

   A. What potential problem did Jesus confront in this passage?

   B. What was his prescription for the problem?

   C. Describe a time you "respected the prescription."

2. Read Luke 4:38–44.

   A. Describe the ministry setting pictured here. What happened?

   B. When did Jesus take a break from his ministering? What did he do?

   C. How did Jesus respond to the people's demands? What does this tell us about our own schedules and the demands we face?

3. Read Luke 5:16.

   A. What regular practice of Jesus is described here?

   B. How frequently did Jesus engage in this practice?

   C. What does this verse suggest to you about your own schedule?

Reawaken the Excitement

1. As you review your S.T.O.R.Y., does the theme of pausing for rest and refreshment show up anywhere? Do you often feel tired? Exhausted? Burned out? Do you take time to rejuvenate your body, soul, and mind? Take some time to track your current record of rest. For the next month, keep a brief journal that records how often you rest, what kind of rest you get, how long it lasts, and how you feel afterward. After the month is done, study this journal and identify

your current habits of rest. Do you get enough rest? The right kind of rest? Does it energize you for your work? Have your spouse or best friend go over your journal with you, and discuss with him or her what you find and any changes you might want to make.

2. Do a study on the concept of "Sabbath" in the Bible. What do you learn about the Sabbath? Who initiated it? Why? What happened when God's people consistently violated it? Why?

Trust
Little Deeds

Cure for the Common Life: Chapter 13

Review the Diagnosis

1. I'm envisioning a reader at the crossroads. One recently impacted by God, perhaps through this book. The divine spark within is beginning to flame. Should you douse it or fan it? Dare you dream that you can make a difference? God's answer would be, "Just do something and see what happens."

   A. Do you think you can make a difference right where God has placed you? Explain.

   B. Dream big. How could your gifts be used to affect the kingdom?

   C. How could you fan your heart's flame to make those dreams a reality?

2. Against a towering giant, a brook pebble seems futile. But God used it to topple Goliath. Compared to the tithes of the wealthy, a widow's coins seem puny. But Jesus used them to inspire us.

A. What towering giant are you facing today? What pebbles do you have at your disposal to attack this giant?

B. Does the widow's gift of coins inspire you? If so, how? If not, why not?

C. How can you pray today to be ready for the mighty thing(s) God might do through you tomorrow?

3. Small deeds can change the world. Sow the mustard seed. Bury the leaven lump. Make the call. Write the check. Organize the committee. Drop some gum from your airplane. Sixty years from now another soldier might follow your example.

A. What call can you make *today* or check can you write *today* that could make a big difference in someone's life?

B. What small deeds from the past have encouraged and inspired you?

C. What kind of example can you leave for others?

4. Moses had a staff. David had a sling. Samson had a jawbone. Rahab had a string. Mary had some ointment. Aaron had a rod. Dorcas had a needle. All were used by God. What do you have?

A. Donating food to a food bank, giving a ride to someone, sending Bibles or study materials to a mission field—what tangible gift can you share?

B. Describe a time when you believe you were used by God.

C. How can you encourage others to use what they have for God?

5. God cures the common life by giving no common life, by offering no common gifts.

A. Do you agree with this statement? Why or why not?

B. How did Halvorsen and Chief Wiggles find a cure for the common life?

C. Describe a seemingly small, common deed someone did for you and its significance in your life.

Respect the Prescription

1. Read Zechariah 4:10.

   A. Why do we often despise the day of small things?

   B. What's wrong with despising the day of small things?

   C. How can we keep from despising the day of small things?

2. Read Matthew 13:31–33.

   A. In what way is the kingdom of heaven like a mustard plant?

   B. In what way is the kingdom of heaven like yeast?

   C. Describe someone you know whose mustard seed was multiplied by God.

3. Read Luke 16:10–12.

   A. What basic principle does Jesus describe in verse 10?

   B. Why is handling small things well so crucial to your future?

   C. Identify the implied warning or threat found in verses 11 and 12. How does this warning/threat impact you?

Reawaken the Excitement

1. Think over the stories you mined to develop your S.T.O.R.Y. What "small things" did God use to lead you into some experience of success or joy? How did he use these small things? The truth is, we

often find patterns not only in the ways our lives unfold but also in the ways God frequently chooses to deal with us. What patterns do you find, if any, in the way God has used small things to impact you and those around you? Make a list of as many of these small things as you can remember, and then describe how they impacted you and your loved ones. Use as many sheets as necessary. After you have finished this exercise, meditate on it for several days, and then start looking for how God might want to use other small things in your life for his glory and your benefit. Pray that he will open your eyes and motivate you to action.

2. Look for people in your life who were faithful in little things and who seemed to be rewarded by God with bigger responsibilities. Set up a time to talk to two or three of these people. What can you learn from their experiences?

DECODE YOUR KID'S CODE

Cure for the Common Life: Chapter 14

Review the Diagnosis

1. Moms and dads face a decision. Make our children in our images? Or release our children to follow their God-given identities?

   A. Are you tempted to try to make your children in your own image? Explain.

   B. How can you help your children find their sweet spots?

   C. How can you best release your children to follow their God-given identities?

2. View each child as a book, not to be written, but to be read.

   A. What does this advice mean to you?

   B. What have you read in your children so far?

   C. How have you responded to what you have read?

3. God prewired your infant. He scripted your toddler's strengths. He set your teen on a trajectory. God gave you an eighteen-year research project. Ask yourself, your spouse, and your friends: what sets this child apart? Childhood tendencies forecast adult abilities.

   A. What sets each of your children apart? How are they distinct individuals?

   B. How have you responded to each of your children's unique personalities?

   C. What do your children's current traits and interests seem to indicate about their possible futures?

4. What about your children? Do you know their hearts? What are their S.T.O.R.Y.'s?

   A. How would you describe each of your children's hearts?

   B. What does each child's S.T.O.R.Y. suggest about how you can best prepare him or her for the future?

   C. If you don't believe you have a good handle on each S.T.O.R.Y., what can you begin doing *today* to improve your handle on it?

5. Study your kids while you can. The greatest gift you can give your children is not your riches, but revealing to them their own.

   A. If you wrote your child's story, what would be the title?

   B. What riches do you see in each of your children?

   C. How have you expressed to your children your delight in their individual riches?

Respect the Prescription

1. Read Proverbs 22:6.

   A. Describe a popular, but incorrect, use of this verse.

   B. What is your responsibility as a parent?

   C. What is your child's responsibility? How do the two intersect?

2. Read Ephesians 6:4.

   A. What are fathers warned against in this verse?

   B. What are fathers instructed to pursue in this verse?

   C. How can you comply with this verse in your family?

3. Read 1 Thessalonians 2:7, 11–12.

   A. What picture does Paul use in verse 7? Why do you think he used this picture?

   B. What picture does Paul use in verse 11? What does it convey?

   C. How do these two pictures work together to show us the best way to prepare our kids for the future?

Reawaken the Excitement

1. Take time to do a preliminary S.T.O.R.Y. for each of your children. Regardless of their current ages, think of specific stories in their lives that seem to illustrate:

   - Their Strengths—what they naturally do to accomplish what they love

   - Their Topics—what things they prefer to work on

- Their Optimal conditions—where and when they are most engaged
- Their Relationships—how they appear to prefer to relate to others
- Their Yes!—the primary outcomes that bring them the most satisfaction and joy

2. Look for opportunities to praise your children individually in specific ways, appropriate to them and their unique giftedness, that will motivate them to pursue God's best for their lives. If you tend to be the critical type, make it a goal to praise your children in specific ways at least three times more often than you criticize them. Keep a scorecard if you have to.

Don't Be Too Big to Do Something Small

Cure for the Common Life: Chapter 15

Review the Diagnosis

1. *There it is, Max, a picture of my plan. Do all you can to push each other to the top.*

   A. How have others helped push you to the top?

   B. How have you helped push others to the top?

   C. In what ways are you most effective in pushing others to the top?

2. God's cure for the common life includes a strong dose of servanthood.

   A. Describe what you think servanthood looks like.

   B. How do you serve at home? At work? At church?

   C. How does servanthood help to cure the common life?

3. A 3:00 a.m. diaper change fits in very few sweet spots. Most S.T.O.R.Y.'s don't feature the strength of garage sweeping. Visiting your sick neighbor might not come naturally to you. Still, the sick need to be encouraged, garages need sweeping, and diapers need changing.

   A. What most tempts you away from serving others?

   B. When do you feel most rewarded in serving others?

   C. What area of neglected service comes to your mind right now?

4. Regardless of your strengths, training, or church tenure, you can . . . *Love the overlooked. . . . Wave a white flag. . . . Every day do something you don't want to do.*

   A. Who in your life is overlooked and needs your love today?

   B. In what area of your life do you most need to "wave a white flag"?

   C. What can you do today that you really don't want to do but probably should?

5. The ascending goat lay down on the path. The other stepped over his back. The first animal then arose and continued his climb to the top. Zwingli observed that the goat made it higher because he was willing to bend lower.

   A. In what ways might you need to bend lower in order to make it higher?

   B. Why is it hard for most of us to bend lower?

   C. Why do you think submission and humility are so important to God?

Respect the Prescription

1. Read 1 Peter 4:10.

   A. How do you use your gift(s) to demonstrate the many faces of God's grace?

   B. How can you use these gifts to serve others?

   C. How does it change your perspective to think of your God-given gifts as expressions of his grace?

2. Read Mark 10:42–45.

   A. What model of leadership does Jesus condemn in verse 42?

   B. What general principle of leadership does he endorse in verses 43–44?

   C. In what practical ways did Jesus demonstrate this teaching in his life?

3. Read Galatians 5:13–14.

   A. How does Christian freedom relate to Christian servanthood?

   B. How is it possible to serve one another but not in love? What does this look like?

   C. How does servanthood relate to this command to love your neighbor as yourself?

Reawaken the Excitement

1. Consider once more the Relationship component of your S.T.O.R.Y. How do you prefer to relate to others? Are you serving them? Would they recognize what you do as service? As you serve them, how would you characterize your attitude? Grateful? Cheerful? Sour?

Disgruntled? Dutiful? Joyful? How could you serve these individuals in ways that you currently are not serving them? Think of two or three ways you could serve these men and women. Then implement at least one of them in the next two weeks.

2. Memorize Galatians 5:13 in a favorite translation of the Bible. Pause frequently throughout the day either to rehearse it in your mind or to say it out loud. Make this the focus of your meditations for at least a week. Then start looking for practical ways to put it into practice in your daily life.

For more information about the Sweet Spot Discovery Guide, contact

People Management International, Inc.
PO Box 1004
Avon, CT 06001-1004

Visit us at
www.peoplemanagement.org

or e-mail us at
sweetspotdiscovery@peoplemanagement.org.

NOTES

Chapter 1: Your Sweet Spot (You Have One!)

1. Frederick Dale Bruner, *Matthew: A Commentary*, vol. 2, *The Churchbook: Matthew 13–28* (Dallas: Word, 1990), 902.

2. Martin Buber, *The Way of Man, According to the Teaching of Hasidism* (London: Routledge Classics, 1994), vi. Jewish theologian Martin Buber writes: "The world is an irradiation of God, but as it is endowed with an independence of existence and striving, it is apt, always and everywhere, to form a crust around itself. Thus, *a divine spark* lives in every thing and being, but each such spark is enclosed by an isolating shell. Only man can liberate it and re-join it with the Origin: by holding holy converse with the thing and using it in a holy manner, that is, so that his intention in doing so remains directed towards God's transcendence. Thus the divine immanence emerges from the exile of the 'shells'" (emphasis mine).

3. "'Red, White & Blue' Students to Present Check to NYC Police, Firemen Nov. 9," Texas A&M University, http://www.tamu.edu/univrel/aggiedaily/news/stories/01/110201-10.

Section 1: Use Your Uniqueness

1. George Washington Carver, as quoted by Paul G. Humber, GodCreatedThat.com, http://www.godcreatedthat.com/Page5.html.

Chapter 2: Unpack Your Bag

1. U.S. Bureau of Labor Statistics, 1998.

2. National Institute for Occupational Safety and Health, "Stress at Work," http://www.cdc.gov/niosh/stresswk.html.

3. Arthur F. Miller Jr. with William Hendricks, *The Power of Uniqueness: How to Become Who You Really Are* (Grand Rapids: Zondervan, 1999), 21.

4. Ellen Galinsky, Stacy S. Kim, and James T. Bond, *Feeling Overworked: When Work Becomes Too Much* (New York: Families and Work Institute, 2001), 11.

5. Nicholas Lore, *The Pathfinder: How to Choose or Change Your Career for a Lifetime of Satisfaction and Success* (New York: Simon & Schuster, 1998), 11.

6. National Institute for Occupational Safety and Health, "Stress at Work."

7. Søren Kierkegaard, *Purity of Heart Is to Will One Thing: Spiritual Preparation for the Office of Confession,* 140, quoted in Miller with Hendricks, *The Power of Uniqueness,* 251.

8. Miller with Hendricks, *The Power of Uniqueness,* 30.

9. Charles R. Swindoll, *The Tale of the Tardy Oxcart and 1,501 Other Stories* (Nashville: Word, 1998), 321–22.

Chapter 3: Read Your Life Backward

1. William Wordsworth, "My Heart Leaps Up When I Behold," Bartelby.com, http://www.bartleby.com/106/286.html.

2. Arthur F. Miller Jr. with William Hendricks, *The Power of Uniqueness: How to Become Who You Really Are* (Grand Rapids: Zondervan, 1999), 46.

3. William Martin, *A Prophet with Honor: The Billy Graham Story* (New York: William Morrow and Co., 1991), 71.

4. Ibid., 57.

5. Not his actual name.

6. Saint Thomas Aquinas, *Summa Theologia,* quoted in Miller with Hendricks, *The Power of Uniqueness,* 250.

7. Any measurement tool is limited in scope. It seeks to place the personality in a grid, box, or grouping. If each person functions in a unique fashion, a test would need a category for each human being. None can provide this.

8. New Testament gift listings are, in my opinion, to be seen as samplings. If they are conclusive, no early church saw the entire list. Rome saw one part, Corinth another, and Peter's audience yet a third. A better option is to see the lists as examples of spiritual skills. Caution, then, is to be taken with spiritual gift inventories. They might *suggest* a gift mix, but can't define one.

Chapter 4: Study Your S.T.O.R.Y.

1. Here is the theme song:

> Come join the RA-AACE
>
> To find your PLA-AACE.
>
> Your bag has CLU-UES,
>
> Packed just for YOU-OUS . . . guys.

Okay—theme songs aren't my sweet spot.

2. Robert Plomin, J. C. DeFries, and G. E. McClearn, *Behavioral Genetics: A Primer* (New York: W. H. Freeman, 1990), 314, quoted in James Hillman, *The*

Soul's Code: In Search of Character and Calling (New York: Random House, 1996), 137.

3. Monica Furlong, *Merton: A Biography* (San Francisco: HarperCollins, 1980), 225.

4. Arthur F. Miller Jr. with William Hendricks, *The Power of Uniqueness: How to Become Who You Really Are* (Grand Rapids: Zondervan, 1999), 55.

5. My thanks to Rick Burgess and Bill "Bubba" Bussey of the *Rick and Bubba Show* from Birmingham, Alabama, for granting permission to use this story.

Chapter 5: Don't Consult Your Greed

1. Linda Kulman, "Our Consuming Interest," *U.S. News & World Report*, June 28–July 5, 2004, 59.

2. Bob Russell with Rusty Russell, *Money: A User's Manual* (Sisters, OR: Multnomah, 1997), 82.

3. Larry Burkett, *Using Your Money Wisely: Guidelines from Scripture* (Chicago: Moody Press, 1986), 76.

4. Kulman, "Our Consuming Interest," 59.

5. Epicurus, GIGA Quotes, http://www.giga-usa.com/quotes/authors/epicurus_a001.htm.

6. Russell with Russell, *Money*, 50–51.

7. Paul Lee Tan, *Encyclopedia of 7,700 Illustrations: Signs of the Times* (Rockville, MD: Assurance Publishers, 1979), 273, #839.

8. Russell with Russell, *Money*, 69.

Chapter 6: Take Big Risks for God

1. Frederick Dale Bruner, *Matthew: A Commentary*, vol. 2, *The Churchbook: Matthew 13–28* (Dallas: Word, 1990), 902.

2. Ibid.

3. C. S. Lewis, *Letters to Malcolm Chiefly on Prayer: Reflections on the Intimate Dialogue between Man and God* (San Diego: Harcourt, 1964), 69.

Chapter 7: Come to the Sweetest Spot in the Universe

1. "Italian Pensioner Seeks Adoption," BBC News, UK Edition, http://news.bbc.co.uk/1/hi/world/europe/3612688.stm.

2. Greg Bensinger, "Gimme a Hug! The 'Cuddle Party' Is New York's Newest Feel-Good-About-Yourself Fad," *New York Daily News*, http://www.nydailynews.com/front/story/211251p-181992c.html.

3. Allaahuakbar.net, "Shirk: The Ultimate Crime," http://www.allaahuakbar.net/shirk/crime.htm.

4. May I applaud those of you who just gave your life to Christ? You now belong
to him! "Whoever accepts and trusts the Son gets in on everything, life
complete and forever!" (John 3:36 MSG). As you begin your new life, remember
three *b*'s: baptism, Bible, belong. Baptism demonstrates and celebrates our
decision to follow Jesus. (See 1 Peter 3:21.) Regular Bible reading guides and
anchors the soul. (See Hebrews 4:12.) Belonging to a church family engages us
with God's children. (See Hebrews 10:25.)

Chapter 9: Join God's Family of Friends

1. "Best Friends for Decades Turn Out to Be Brothers," Channel 8 News,
http://www.newschannel8.com/global/story.asp?s=599530&ClientType.

2. These words appear in the New Century Version.

3. C. S. Lewis, Thinkexist.com, http://en.thinkexist.com/search/
searchQuotation.asp?search=friendship+is+born+.

4. John MacArthur Jr., *The MacArthur New Testament Commentary: Ephesians*
(Chicago: Moody Press, 1986), 152.

5. John 13:34; Romans 12:10; 16:17; Galatians 6:2; Hebrews 3:13; James 5:16;
Hebrews 13:2

Chapter 10: Tank Your Reputation

1. Scot McKnight, *The Jesus Creed: Loving God, Loving Others* (Brewster, MA:
Paraclete Press, 2004), 77.

2. The Jewish confession of faith, comprising Deuteronomy 6:4–9; 11:13–21; and
Numbers 15:37–41.

Section 3: Every Day of Your Life

1. John C. Maxwell, *The 21 Indispensable Qualities of a Leader: Becoming the Person
Others Will Want to Follow* (Nashville: Thomas Nelson, 1999), 16–18.

Chapter 11: Take Your Job and Love It

1. Rick Warren, *Growing Spiritually at Work,* pt. 1 of *Beyond Success to Significance,*
audiotape from Encouraging Word, PO Box 6080-388, Mission Viejo, CA
92690.

2. Dan Miller, *48 Hours to the Work You Love* (Nashville: Broadman & Holman,
2005), 48.

3. Michael Card, *The Life,* compact disc, Sparrow, card insert. Used by permission.

4. Haddon Robinson, "By the Sweat of Your Brow," pt. 2, *PreachingToday.com,*
http://www.preachingtoday.com.

Chapter 12: Pause on Purpose

1. My thanks to Ernie Johnson Jr. for allowing me to use this story.
2. My thanks to Richard Wellock (rmwellock@aol.com) for his insights into exploring individuals' unique giftedness and relating it to career choices.
3. Richard J. Foster, *Celebration of Discipline: The Path to Spiritual Growth*, 20th anniversary ed. (San Francisco: HarperSanFrancisco, 1998), 15.
4. Eugene H. Peterson, *Working the Angles: The Shape of Pastoral Integrity* (Grand Rapids: William B. Eerdmans, 1987), 56–57.

Chapter 13: Trust LITTLE Deeds

1. "The Candy Bomber," http://www.konnections.com/airlift/candy.htm.
2. Frederick Dale Bruner, *Matthew: A Commentary*, vol. 2, *The Churchbook: Matthew 13–28* (Dallas: Word, 1990), 504.
3. Elmer Bendiner, *The Fall of Fortresses: A Personal Account of the Most Daring—and Deadly—American Air Battles of World War II* (New York: G. P. Putnam's Sons, 1980), 138–39.
4. "Chief Wiggles (2003, Operation Give)," Operation Give, www.operationgive.org.
5. John Wesley, http://www.myquotations.net/?QuoteID-58602.

Chapter 14: Decode Your Kid's Code

1. Charles R. Swindoll, *You and Your Child* (Nashville: Thomas Nelson, 1977), 21.
2. R. G. Collingwood, *An Autobiography* (Oxford: Oxford University Press, 1939), 3–4, quoted in James Hillman, *The Soul's Code: In Search of Character and Calling* (New York: Random House, 1996), 14–15.
3. Howard Reich, *Van Cliburn: A Biography* (Nashville: Thomas Nelson, 1993), quoted in Hillman, *The Soul's Code*, 70.
4. John Ruskin, http://www.myquotations.net/?QuoteID-47716.
5. Paul D. Colford, *The Rush Limbaugh Story: Talent on Loan from God* (New York: St. Martin's Press, 1993), 12, quoted in Hillman, *The Soul's Code*, 106.
6. Omar N. Bradley Jr. and Clay Blair, *A General's Life: An Autobiography* (New York: Simon and Schuster, 1983), quoted in Hillman, *The Soul's Code*, 105.
7. Golda Meir, *My Life* (New York: Putnam, 1975), 38–39, quoted in Hillman, *The Soul's Code*, 20.

Chapter 15: Don't Be Too Big to Do Something Small

1. Not his actual name
2. Lynn Anderson, "Portrait of a Servant," (sermon, date unknown).

3. Paul Lee Tan, *Encyclopedia of 7,700 Illustrations: Signs of the Times* (Rockville, MD: Assurance Publishers, 1979), 1370–71, #6124.

4. M. Norvel Young with Mary Hollingsworth, *Living Lights, Shining Stars: Ten Secrets to Becoming the Light of the World* (West Monroe, LA: Howard Publishing, 1997), 7.

5. Young with Hollingsworth, *Living Lights, Shining Stars*, 11–12.

Conclusion: Sweet Spots: Two People Who Found Theirs

1. Richard E. Stearns, president, World Vision U.S., personal conversation.

2. Lori Neal, graduate student, personal conversation.

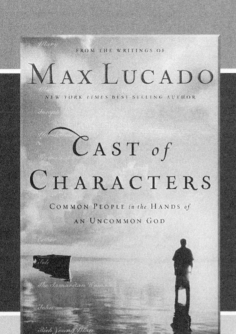

The Bestseller Collection

Fall 2008

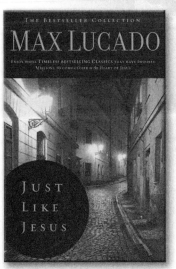

These affordable, yet high-quality hardcover books are priced for sharing the timeless and timely message of Max Lucado with friends, family, and co-workers. Or perhaps to introduce a fan to a volume previously missed, or to

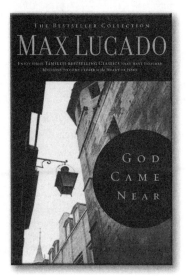

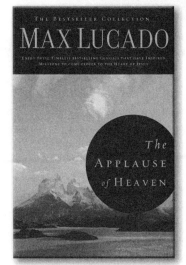

Coming Soon in Summer 2009:

He Still Moves Stones · *In the Eye of the Storm* · *When Christ Comes*

# of Max Lucado

Winter 2009

connect Max's amazing message of grace with someone brand new.
   Join us as we collect these jewels from the treasure box of Max's million-copy bestsellers for a fitting display of insight and inspiration.

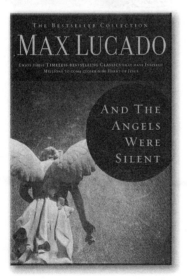

For more information, visit:

www.ThomasNelson.com · *www.MaxLucado.com*

A LIFE-CHANGING MESSAGE FROM AMERICA'S PASTOR

Embark on a journey of hope and encouragement for daily living with Max Lucado as he unpacks the timeless message of John 3:16.

If you know nothing of the Bible, start here. If you know everything in the Bible, return here. It's a twenty-six word parade of hope: beginning with God, ending with life and urging us to do the same.

HE LOVES.
HE GAVE.
WE BELIEVE.
WE LIVE.

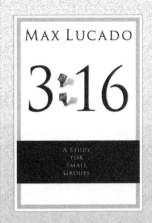

If 9/11 are the numbers of terror and despair, then 3:16 are the numbers of hope. Best-selling author Max Lucado leads readers through a word-by-word study of John 3:16, the passage that he calls the "Hope Diamond" of scripture. The study includes 12 lessons that are designed to work with both the trade book and the Indelible DVD for a multi-media experience.

Listen to the message of 3:16 in your home or take it on the road. This CD makes the perfect gift for the family or friends you want to hear the hope found in John 3:16.

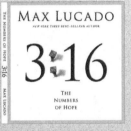

3:16 is also available in Spanish, Portuguese, German, Swedish, Dutch, Korean, Japanese, and Chinese.

GOD'S GREAT BIG LOVE FOR ME

With colored beads built right in, this board book is the perfect book to teach the verse and meaning behind John 3:16 to preschool children.
Available February 2008

3:16 – THE NUMBERS OF HOPE TEEN EDITION

Max offers his unique and simple storytelling for this important message while Tricia Goyer writes teen responses to Max's message, guiding teens to fully understand how this verse can impact their lives. From confession to praise, these responses are sure to bring an insightful look into the personal faith of teens.
Available February 2008

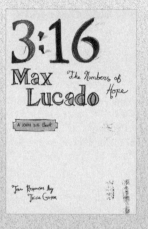

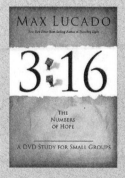

A DVD FOR SMALL GROUP STUDY

This is a kit designed and priced specifically for small groups. It will include a copy of the study guide for small groups, an evangelism booklet, the Indelible DVD, and a CD-ROM with facilitator's guide information and promotional material.